A Practical Guide on Implementing
SUGGESTION SYSTEMS

Amanda,

This publication was meant as a modest beginning. Let's work from here. Good luck

A E Marx

Andrew E Marx
2 August 1993

A Practical Guide on Implementing SUGGESTION SYSTEMS

❖

ANDREW E MARX
Professor of Business Economics
University of Pretoria

1992
JUTA & CO, LTD

First published in 1992

PO Box 14373, Kenwyn 7790

ISBN 0 7021 2794 9

Printed and bound in South Africa by
The Rustica Press, Ndabeni, Cape.

D1399

This book is dedicated to my good friend

RIEL CILLIERS

and to

ONS EERSTE VOLKSBANK (PTY) LTD
(PRETORIA)

Contents

ANNEXURES

1. INTRODUCTION

Man's worldly possessions and his aspirations for the future are the results of people's ideas. Ideas are not the sole right of the intellectual, but often originate with the not so intelligent. However, having the skills and ability is of no consequence without the opportunity or means whereby these can be realised. What is required is some mechanism within an organisation through which the employee can present his ideas to management.

While the organisation strives toward supplying high quality goods and services and the optimal use of inputs, the need to find alternate ways of controlling cost, improving productivity and performance becomes of major importance. One of the oldest management tools available which fulfils all of the above requirements and at the same time offers the employee the advantage of being able to 'cash in' in terms of financial enrichment and other intangible benefits such as individual recognition and work satisfaction, is nothing other than the suggestion system. The suggestion system has been given a variety of labels, for example 'innovation programme', 'management innovation programme', 'management idea programme' and many others, but to avoid any confusion, it will from here on be referred to as the suggestion scheme.

A suggestion scheme affords the employee an opportunity to make a positive contribution towards improving the performance levels within the organisation. Ultimately, both the employer and employee benefit from the suggestion scheme.

The concept of rewarding employees for their suggestions is not new. As early as 1857, although it wasn't intended as a suggestion scheme, a worker at the Birmingham Glassworks in England was awarded £10 by the firm of Chance Bros Ltd for developing a glass-flattening fork. William Denny of the William Denny Ship Building Co. is regarded as the founder of the formal suggestion scheme. In 1880 he came to the conclusion that the experience which his employees had could help to improve the business. He invited his employees to submit to him their ideas on ways of improving the business.

The first formal suggestion scheme in the USA was implemented in 1894 by the well known NCR company. In South Africa, a suggestion scheme was implemented in 1908 by the then Zuid-Afrikaanse Spoorweë which, up to March 1982 had received 104 224 suggestions, of which 18 708 were implemented. These results are insignificant considering that it took place over a 74-year period, but on a more positive note, most of these suggestions would have been lost had there been no suggestion scheme. On 1 September 1915, an official suggestion scheme began at the then Department of Posts. These schemes are possibly the two oldest in the RSA. Since 1949, when Iscor began with a suggestion scheme, the concept has gained ground. Iscor in particular, has done pioneering work in this field.

Although the concept of the suggestion scheme became known during the second half of the 19th century, it was only applied, with limited success, at the beginning of the 20th century. In general, the growth of suggestion schemes was slow. However, only with the outbreak of World War Two, governments and organisations realised that they had to make the best use of all production factors, including the knowledge and experience of employees, in order to survive. Thus, 1942 proved to be the watershed year for the suggestion scheme, which then gathered momentum.

The majority of South African companies have had an apathetic attitude toward suggestion schemes in spite of the considerable successes achieved by some organisations locally and internationally. A suggestion scheme is not a panacea for all organisational ailments but it can be an extremely useful management tool when it comes to improving overall performance.

2. DEFINITION OF A SUGGESTION SCHEME

A suggestion scheme can be defined as a formal procedure which encourages employees to think creatively about their work and work environment and to produce ideas which will benefit the organisation, and for which they will receive specific recognition if the ideas are used.

The criteria for qualification as a formal scheme are the following:

- The accepted suggestions must relate to a specific problem, a potential problem or an opportunity to improve a process or a situation.
- A suggestion must provide the solution to the problem or potential problem. A complaint about an existing situation which does not address the solution is not regarded as a suggestion. Where an opportunity is pointed out, a possible strategy to utilise it should be given.
- Suggestions should be in writing, preferably on a prescribed form.
- The suggestion must be signed by the employee, even in circumstances where the employee wishes to remain anonymous.
- The written suggestion must be received and registered by the suggestion office, who must record the time and date of receipt.
- The scheme must be recognised and accepted by top management.

A suggestion box which is strategically placed and which is emptied regularly, does not necessarily constitute a formal suggestion scheme. Unsuccessful suggestion schemes are as a result of the informality of suggestion boxes. The recommendation is to eliminate these and to hand in suggestions directly or use the internal post to send them to the suggestion office.

3. DEFINITION OF A SUGGESTION

A suggestion can be defined as a proposal to bring about change. This does not necessarily imply that a suggestion has to be something new. Essentially the objective of a suggestion is to improve a current situation.

A suggestion is a written proposal that could be a strategy, a design or an idea to change a situation in order to improve that situation.

Suggestions fall into four general categories:

- Improvement of systems, methods and processes, tools and equipment, working conditions, packaging and labels, materials and provision of materials, scheduling procedures and the use of by-products.
- Improvement in the quality of products and/or services.
- Reduction of costs or elimination of waste.
- Safety measures and safety aids.

Suggestions can be divided into two groups according to the calculability of the results achieved.

3.1 Tangible suggestions

Tangible suggestions are those whose results can be measured in quantifiable terms. A precise financial value can be attributed to the suggestion and the net saving can thus be accurately determined. These types of suggestions have definite tangible advantages for the organisation.

3.2 Intangible suggestions

Intangible or non-quantifiable suggestions are those whose results cannot be precisely or scientifically quantified. Examples are the improvement of safety, an improved company image, more favourable working conditions, a higher employee morale, improved service and co-operation. It is difficult to quantify saving in these cases.

4. AIM OF A SUGGESTION SCHEME

4.1 Creative thoughts

The most important aim of a suggestion scheme is to promote and encourage employees to become creative and constructive thinkers so that management can reap the benefits of their initiative, ability and resourcefulness.

4.2 Working relationships

Suggestion systems can also improve employer–employee relationships. This occurs as a result of employee participation in the creation/development of activities that lead to improved working conditions and processes, equipment and general neatness of the working environment. The close co-operation between the participating parties develops into an improved relationship. Suggestion schemes also fit into the spirit of participative management which is becoming an increasingly important management style.

4.3 Interest and loyalty

Because employees are compensated for suggestions and become indirectly involved in the decision-making process, their interest in the organisation's activities can be stimulated. This usually leads to a better team spirit and a greater sense of loyalty towards the organisation. The suggestion scheme has a motivational effect which leads to a reduction in labour turnover because the employees feel part of a larger team which they will not readily give up.

4.4 Compensation

A further aim of the suggestion scheme is to compensate employees financially or otherwise for worthwhile suggestions. The higher one moves in Maslow's Hierarchy of Needs, the less important financial rewards become and other methods of recognition take on more significance. Regardless of the level at which the employee finds himself, recognition of a suggestion remains essential. Employees do not win recognition for a suggestion, they earn it.

5. ADVANTAGES OF A SUGGESTION SCHEME

In addition to the objectives associated with suggestion schemes, there are definite benefits for both the organisation and the employee.

5.1 Organisational benefits

5.1.1 Financial savings

One of the most important benefits of a suggestion scheme is the financial saving achieved in the form of cost reduction and cost avoidance. Suggestion systems *seldom make a loss*, particularly when they are evaluated over a period exceeding three years. A successful suggestion scheme is, therefore, not a cost — it is an investment.

A formal scheme can result in savings and cost advantages that far outweigh the cost of the system. Research has shown that on average the return per rand expended is approximately R6 per year. This calculation was based on the first-year saving only, and when extended over a number of years has a tendency to multiply. The average life-span of a suggestion which has been implemented is between four and seven years.

5.1.2 Improvement in morale

Unless extensive attitude surveys are conducted, improvement in the morale of the employees as a result of suggestion systems and the related benefits to the organisation are difficult to measure. The submission and adoption of a suggestion may encourage a sense of employee achievement and result in more motivated employees with a greater interest in the growth and development of the organisation. Employee morale can also be improved when the suggestion system serves as a safety valve allowing employees an opportunity to propose constructive solutions to problems which would otherwise have remained complaints and a source of worker irritation.

5.1.3 Central and peripheral problems

All organisations have so-called central and peripheral problems. It is impossible for management to analyse all these problems to the finest detail. Management is kept busy with central issues which are fundamental to the existence of the organisation, for example, production and marketing problems. The smaller peripheral problems which the employees experience are, to a large extent, unknown to management. The larger the organisation, the greater the gap between central and peripheral problems. The suggestion system may, from time to time, assist management in becoming aware of the smaller brim problems which will give them insight and understanding of matters which would normally be neglected. Generally, the highlighting of the smaller problems should not waste management's time as the suggestion identifies the problem and, at the same time, proffers a possible solution.

5.1.4 Improvements of products and services

Suggestions often result in an improvement in the products of the organisation, whether services or consumer goods. This could help the organisation gain an edge over its competitors, resulting in a constant or even an increased market share. This applies to both local and international markets. (The implication is that there are national and organisational benefits.)

5.1.5 A resurgence process

Encouragement of new ideas by employees leads to a resurgence of the organisation. Although the organisation is dynamic in the sense that it experiences continual resurgence, it never achieves perfection. Many changes may be advantageous but could also result in new problems. The resurgence process never reaches saturation point, so there will always be a need for the existence of suggestion schemes.

5.1.6 Reduction of labour turnover

A suggestion scheme can lead to a reduction in the labour turnover rate as it tends to create an esprit de corps among the employees. The resulting increase in loyalty towards the organisation often causes employees to reconsider their tasks and develop new ways to improve and change their work. A decrease in the turnover rate not only results in higher employee moral and a sound team spirit, it also has direct and indirect financial implications associated with replacing employees (training, recruitment, etc.).

5.1.7 Improved communication

A suggestion scheme provides an additional medium of communication — a channel between the various levels of employees within the organisation. Obviously, a suggestion scheme is not a solution to poor communication, it is merely an additional communication channel. Every time an employee proposes a suggestion, whether it is accepted or not, management becomes aware of employee-related issues while the worker is aware that his suggestion is at last being evaluated.

5.1.8 Reduced resistance to change

Since the proposal to change originated with the employees, the changes will be more readily accepted. As a result, the resistance-to-change factor is lessened to a large degree. Employees feel that they have to make their ideas succeed, they being the ones who proposed the change.

5.1.9 Improved management–employee relations

A well-administered suggestion scheme which has the acceptance of the employees can lead to improved labour relations. Improved management–employee relations and team spirit will be the net result.

5.1.10 A management tool

An advantage of suggestion schemes which is often not realised is that it provides management with an additional tool. These schemes provide the opportunity to put the initiative and the intelligence of the employees to work to the advantage of the organisation. In addition, supervision becomes far easier as the employees become more cost-conscious.

5.1.11 A safer work environment

Suggestions contribute to safer working conditions and an improved working environment with cleaner, neater and safer facilities. Good maintenance of the work place takes on a new significance especially where dangerous equipment is being used.

5.2 Employee benefits

The organisation is not the only one to benefit from the use of a suggestion scheme. The employee also receives the following benefits:

5.2.1 Additional income

Employees are provided with a way to increase their take-home pay by submitting successful suggestions — the greater the volume of acceptable suggestions, the more chances to increase their income.

5.2.2 Recognition and motivation

Recognition, which is an excellent motivation, plays a vital role in the suggestion scheme. Employees who receive both financial and peer recognition for their suggestions will be highly motivated. The recognition earned from a scheme is an important means of satisfaction of higher level needs and serves as a strong motivator.

5.2.3 An outlet mechanism

Frustration with unresolved problems often cause irritation, but providing a suggestion scheme where the individual can possibly solve the problem himself will help to ease the irritation. The employee's self-development is enhanced further by innovative and creative suggestions.

5.2.4 Prestige

When suggestions are accepted the employee is provided with the opportunity to belong to an elite group, the group which truly contributes towards the success of the organisation. Since status is one of the individual's higher order needs, it is a strong motivational factor.

5.2.5 Promotion

Provided sufficient suggestions are submitted, recognition and development are inevitable. Suggestions may even determine the employee's future career. Accepted suggestions furthermore provide opportunities for self-development. Employees not only receive special recognition for suggestions; management also becomes aware of the suggestor's special talents and he could be singled out for promotion.

6. DISADVANTAGES OF SUGGESTION SCHEMES

It would be untrue to say that there are no disadvantages involved in operating suggestion system. What must be emphasised is that all the disadvantages stem from the human element. With the correct handling and a deeper insight into the suggestion scheme, they can be turned into positive advantages.

6.1 Misunderstanding and dissatisfaction

Maladministration and a lack of management support are two factors which easily lead to misunderstanding and dissatisfaction amongst employees. This tends to negate advantages of suggestion systems. A single element could have such a negative impact that the entire employee programme and, ultimately the employees productivity is severely affected. Paragraphs 7.1 and 7.11 will show that management support, efficient administration and processing are absolutely essential for the success of suggestion schemes. If these major ingredients are absent, the suggestion scheme will be doomed to failure from the very beginning. Establishing and commencing a scheme without the necessary management support and infrastructure is to court disaster.

6.2 Management–Employee relations

The degree of success of the suggestion scheme is proportional to the amount of involvement of management in the scheme. Employees often sense that management is using the scheme as a smoke-screen and is merely paying lip service to the scheme. In this event, the management–employee relationship will become severely strained. This problem can be overcome if the organisational climate is conducive to suggestion schemes, implying that management fully supports the scheme. (See paragraph 7.10.)

6.3 Individualism

The very nature of a traditional suggestion scheme encourages individualism at the expense of team spirit, since every employee is working for his own pocket. Ideas are not shared easily with colleagues, possibly for fear of idea theft, especially when financial awards are in the offing. The information flow between colleagues breaks down because of this inherent fear. It can place a severe strain on relationships when co-operation between group members is essential, thereby affecting the organisation as a whole.

The organisation can overcome the negative effect by stressing *Group Suggestions* and the important role they play. Individualism will tend to fade. It has been found that groups are inclined to collaborate on suggestions with the result that more suggestions result than if the group members acted individually. Cross-pollination of ideas is the main contributor to the increase in ideas.

6.4 Rejection by the group

An employee who is a high volume suggestor is often branded as a 'rate-buster' by his colleagues because of the individualistic nature of the traditional scheme. They feel threatened by his actions, fearing for their jobs. Peer pressure is brought to bear in an attempt to get the suggestion to conform to the group norm. If the suggestor refuses to conform he/she may be rejected by the group. *Group suggestions* can alleviate the problem as the group participates in the suggestion and shares the recognition.

6.5 Irregularities

Good management practice will ensure that the scheme is run fairly with no irregularities and malpractices. If any malpractices do occur, they are usually cases of unjust enrichment by ineligible employees. A common example involves an employee who is ineligible, passing on a suggestion to a friend who is eligible and agreeing to share the award. Although this will not cause the downfall of the scheme, it can affect the productivity of the group. Sound *management principles* will ensure that these problems are minimised. Making the eligibility as wide as possible also overcomes this problem.

6.6 Taxation of additional income

Financial awards are regarded by the Receiver of Revenue as being additional income and, as such, are fully taxable in the hands of the recipient. In most cases, the burden of the taxation is borne by the suggestor, but it is contended that the organisation should bear the burden and that the suggestor be awarded a net sum equivalent to the full amount of the award. Although it appears that the organisation pays this tax on behalf of the employee, in reality the Receiver of Revenue pays because the total compensation costs, that is the net compensation plus the tax thereon, is shown as expenditure in the financial statements, and as such is fully deductible from the organisation's profits, thus reducing the tax.

7. CONDITIONS FOR SUCCESSFUL IMPLEMENTATION

A number of conditions are necessary to ensure the successful implementation of a suggestion scheme. Some of these conditions are outlined below.

7.1 The commitment and involvement of top management

One of the most crucial factors which spell success is the commitment to, and the involvement of top management in the suggestion scheme. The scheme needs management's approval for the funds to establish and maintain the necessary infrastructure as well as the award system, which is vital to the success of the scheme.

Top management, having made the commitment to the scheme, must ensure that all levels of management are familiar with and understand the concepts of the scheme in order for it to become a part of the management objectives. Supervisors must be trained to give recognition instead of criticism for suggestions emanating from their subordinates. In many cases they may well have to help the suggestors with their ideas.

7.2 The development of an infrastructure

Management should provide a budget which is sufficient to fund the system. This should make provision for funds for the award system, stationery and other operating expenses (including the salary of an administrator and additional overheads that should be added to the duties of an existing post), the appointment of a suggestion committee and the printing of publicity material.

Suggestion scheme success is largely dependent on the efficiency of its infrastructure and is proportional to the funds spent, e.g. R10 for every R1 spent.

7.3 The enthusiasm of the co-ordinator and the suggestion committee

The administrator and the suggestion committee bear responsibility for the management and maintenance of the scheme. Their ability and attitude are prime factors in maintaining continued interest of supervisors and employees in the scheme. The ability of the administrator and the suggestion committee is determined by his/their knowledge of the subject and his/their ability to work with people. Great care must be taken by management when selecting the persons who are to be made responsible for the scheme.

7.4 The supervisor's involvement

Supervisors/line managers/foremen are often the most important link in the suggestion system. Without their support it is hardly likely that subordinates will come up with new ideas. If there is an air of negativity it will pervade down to the subordinates with the result that participation dwindles. The supervisor's role is an important aspect in the success of the scheme. The following indicate why:

- Suggestions originating in a specific area are usually referred to the supervisor. He decides whether the suggestion will be accepted or implemented, especially when it relates to his particular area of supervision. If he suppresses all the initiatives of his subordinates, he will be unable to motivate them to participate.
- Because the supervisor is engaged in evaluating the suggestions, he is instrumental in determining the advantages or savings of the idea. The value of the saving will also determine the award value and if the suggestion is unfairly treated it will result in a demotivated group of suggestors.
- The supervisor is the communication channel through which employees can exchange and submit ideas to management. If the supervisor blocks this channel, the suggestions cannot be taken further and management will remain unaware of these ideas.
- The supervisor who maintains a good relationship with his subordinates will be able to motivate them to submit an unending flow of suggestions.

Any idea, no matter how small or unrealistic, should nevertheless receive fair consideration. Investigation of each and every suggestion becomes part and parcel of the supervisor's duties and by fulfilling these duties he will, at the same time, encourage his subordinates to keep bringing forth suggestions. However, all is not a bed of roses, because some supervisors discourage suggestions from subordinates for the following reasons:

- The fear that good suggestions may overshadow the supervisor's own performance.
- Supervisors do not set aside the time and effort to evaluate suggestions.
- Some supervisors feel that suggestions point out problems which they should have noticed.
- Fearing the unknown, supervisors often require training in the evaluation of suggestions and unless they are trained, they will avoid the scheme at all costs.
- The recognition and awards which the employee receives can have the opposite effect on the supervisor, causing a certain amount of resentment.
- Doubts may exist in the minds of supervisors as to the real value of suggestion schemes.
- Employee involvement is one of the objectives of a suggestion scheme with the result that the supervisor may be led to believe that he is excluded from participating in the scheme.

Most of the resistance and resentment results from lack of knowledge, not only as far as the supervisor/line manager/foreman is concerned, but also the top management of the organisation.

The following rules should be followed if supervisor involvement is sought and to create a positive attitude:

- Top management should make public their support for the scheme. This organisation-wide declaration will involve the supervisors and generate their support since they, too, are part of management.
- Top management should include supervisors in the planning, policy-making, co-ordination and controlling of the sugges-

tion scheme. The supervisor must not only feel that he is involved in the programme but must also feel part of it. The *'your programme'* must be changed to *'our programme'*. A problem may arise when new supervisors who did not take part in the planning of the scheme are appointed. A well-structured induction programme for the new supervisor should include this aspect. The new supervisor must be made to believe in the scheme and the related success. Nothing is more convincing than good results, which emphasises the point that a suggestion scheme must therefore be result-orientated.

- Top management should hold the supervisors responsible for the operation and success of the scheme after the correct orientation and briefing as to the nature and advantages of the scheme has been given. This will involve them in the management of the programme.
- Top management should ensure that a copy of the suggestor's idea forms part of the relevant supervisor's personnel record when evaluating work achievement. The supervisor stands to gain by way of acknowledgement for the high level of participation of his subordinates. The verbal, written and financial acknowledgement will serve to motivate the supervisor to achieve even greater heights.
- Supervisors should encourage ideas and suggestions from subordinates. A supervisor who is indifferent to the employee's suggestions and ideas, becomes impatient with the suggestor, or who is too busy to listen, is building a wall between him and his subordinates. The supervisor should reverse roles with the suggestor, placing himself in the suggestor's position and from this, decide on what action to take.
- Give credit where credit is due. A supervisor who practices this credo will engender loyalty. This practice is not only sound as far as management practice is concerned, but is also indicative of a good supervisor.
- Management should ensure that all suggestions received are appraised and evaluated, no matter how small and insignifi-

cant they may seem. Many ideas may consist of small improvements but they are a start to creative thinking. A small improvement is better than no improvement at all. A supervisor, who is looking for the big money-saving idea may overlook the smaller ideas from employees and, as a result, discourage them from submitting further suggestions. It is far better to obtain a few comprehensive suggestions than none at all.

- Whenever suggestions are evaluated and rejected the supervisor should provide specific and valid reasons why they were not accepted. The suggestor is entitled to know these reasons. Moreover, the supervisor should not disclaim responsibility for rejecting the suggestion and shift the blame onto the suggestion committee or any other person. The employees will soon realise what is happening and the supervisor is likely to lose the respect of his subordinates.
- The supervisor should be on hand to assist the suggestor with the completion of his suggestion, especially where there is a high percentage of illiteracy among the work force. This type of support is indicative of sound supervisory qualities.
- Employee suggestions should, at all times, be respected by supervisors. The time and energy vested in these suggestions and their implementation make them very important to the employee. Until he is told to the contrary, he will be expecting recognition for his idea.
- Participation in a suggestion scheme is a gradual process and requires constant promotion, publicity and word of mouth to keep it alive. Successful schemes require the same sort of support. Employees need to be motivated to submit suggestions about their work. Ideas will bring about increased productivity. The supervisor must ensure that any deterrents to submitting suggestions are removed and, if there is employee resistance, the supervisor's task is to break it down and convert that energy into submitting suggestions.

The involvement of the supervisor is thus essential for the success of the suggestion scheme.

7.5 Employee involvement

Good ideas seldom result from indiscriminate change. They are more likely to emanate from people who are actively on the lookout for ideas. It stands to reason that employees are hardly likely to come up with ideas which could result in their being retrenched. It must be abundantly clear that no one will lose his job as a result of a suggestion.

An organisation needs to sell its suggestion system to the employees since they are the ones who need convincing of the financial rewards which await them.

The following are some ideas which can be used to *'sell'* a suggestions scheme.

- A brochure which includes an explanation of the scheme, as well as a flow diagram of the system starting from the submission of the suggestion to its acceptance and the award or rejection of the suggestion (see figure 2 on page 59). The use of a multilingual brochure has a decided advantage.
- A letter from top management which outlines the scheme.
- An article in the internal personnel news sheet containing full details of the scheme.
- The use of posters, which should be changed on a regular basis to maintain interest.
- Audiovisual aids (videos and slide programmes).
- The annual budget should make provision for awards, personnel and advertising costs.
- Keynote speeches at every opportunity.
- A specially designed suggestion form with the rules of the scheme on the reverse of the form (for an example see annexure 1/2 on page 87).

Employees, senior management and supervisory involvement are the three essential elements which a suggestion scheme requires to function successfully.

7.6 The suggestion scheme policy

There should be a clearly defined policy which leaves little room for personal judgements and arguments, thereby reducing favouritism and dissatisfaction. Every aspect of the scheme should be clearly defined so that employees are left in no doubt as to what is expected of them and what they can expect from the organisation in return (for an example see annexure 1 on page 80).

7.7 The awareness programme

An awareness programme is essential at the start of any new scheme. Employees who are potential suggestors should be informed as to what the new programme embraces, what it offers them, what it offers the organisation and when the programme begins.

A publicity programme is as important to the existing scheme as it is for a new scheme. Employees should be reminded on a continual basis of the importance and benefits of a suggestion scheme. One of the best ways of eliciting ideas is to ask the employees for them.

The publicity programme should emphasise the awards paid to suggestors and publicise the award ceremonies. Employees should be made aware of the awards which are actually being made. If someone doesn't see what happens to submitted suggestions, he will lose interest in the scheme. The importance of a publicity programme for an established scheme cannot be stressed sufficiently.

A publicity programme may comprise certain aspects, for example, a book of rules that outline the policy, a guide for supervisors, a brochure for the employees, an induction brochure outlining the scheme, circulars, posters, salary packet inserts, occasional speeches and newspaper and magazine articles.

A suggestion scheme should be dynamic and vibrantly alive which is why a continual awareness programme is of great importance.

7.8 Exercising patience

One of the essential requirements is patience on the part of management. Suggestion schemes seldom become a roaring success overnight. It takes time to gain recognition and acceptability among the employees and only then will the benefits begin accruing to both the organisation and the employees. Once the scheme begins to gain credibility, the suggestion input levels begin to rise. Management should realise that a suggestion scheme is not a panacea for all the ills of the organisation.

Taking into account the pioneering role played by the evaluators, particularly with a new scheme, the time taken to reach a point where an effective evaluation of the scheme can be made could be anything up to three years.

Management should exercise patience and not expect tangible and meaningful results within a period of one year.

7.9 A proper system of compensation

Employees cannot be forced into participating in the suggestion scheme. It is a purely voluntary activity and there has to be an incentive for an employee to participate. When the incentive is small, participation is not that good, employees are reluctant to submit their suggestions. The awareness of the awards will have an effect on the success of the scheme, which makes the publicity which the award ceremony receives an important factor.

Awards need not be financial in nature. There are two types of awards, namely:

- Merit or recognition awards, such as certificates, pins or lapel buttons, or a letter from top management; and
- cash and other tangible awards such as articles, paid tours and paid holidays.

The generally accepted basis for calculating the financial award is the savings achieved in the first year.

The knowledge that extra effort in developing suggestions could make it worth the employees' time plays an important role in the success of the scheme.

7.10 The correct organisational climate

In an organisation which has a predominantly autocratic management style, a suggestion scheme is less likely to succeed, the reason being that the autocrat is insensitive to the ideas of others. The suggestion scheme is a management tool that involves the employee and is therefore a tool for participative management. If, on the other hand, management is not in favour of participative management, the suggestion scheme will be worthless. Before any measure of success can be achieved with a suggestion scheme, there must be some indication of an attitude change towards participative management throughout the entire organisation.

7.11 Orderly administration and processing

One of the reasons why suggestion schemes struggle is the administrative delays sometimes experienced. When suggestions are delayed, employees get the impression that the organisation views their ideas as worthless. An early acknowledgement of receipt of the suggestion is absolutely essential. Suggestion boxes (if used) should be cleared on a daily basis and the suggestor should be advised as soon as possible.

Another two discouraging elements are the length of time taken to evaluate a suggestion and delay in paying the awards. The suggestor may begin to have doubts about the system particularly when his idea has been used. These two elements should be regarded as serious demotivators. Reliable evaluations are essential and the amount of time devoted to the evaluation should be as short as possible. The suggestor must be notified of the results as soon as possible.

Part of the administrative function is the maintenance of a register which allows strict control over suggestions. All suggestions are treated fairly on a first-come basis and when evaluations are unnecessarily delayed they can be followed up. The register simplifies the compilation of statistics for management reports. Computerisation of the register has simplified the registration process and facilitates the extraction of data.

The register should contain, inter alia, the following data:

- The number of eligible personnel.
- The number of suggestions submitted.
- The number of employees who participated.
- The total number of suggestions adopted.
- The total estimated savings as a result of suggestions adopted.
- The total amount paid out as awards.
- The total number of suggestions in process.

Armed with this information, it will be possible to present management with meaningful reports (see annexure 4/2 on page 115).

7.12 Training of suggestors

Although training is not a prerequisite for the success of a suggestion scheme, it does contribute to faster growth and a quicker return on investment. In cases where training is not given, information can be distributed by leaflets.

New-employee induction and orientation programmes should include an overview of the suggestion scheme. If at any time training is deemed necessary for implementing a scheme, the emphasis should fall on the awareness of a problem, the analysis of the problem and the formulation of a solution.

Employees should be given examples of the types of ideas and suggestions during the training. It is often necessary to teach the suggestor to express his idea in writing on the prescribed form or by any other means. Employees should be made aware that there are several basic aspects which lead to improved suggestions. These aspects are the following:

- ❑ Learn as much as possible about the job and the equipment needed to perform it.
- ❑ Keep abreast of the latest technological developments in the relevant field by reading as much technical literature as is available.
- ❑ Because something was done in a certain way in the past, that is no reason to continue doing in the same way.
- ❑ Question everything and then determine whether there isn't a better way of doing it.
- ❑ An idea should never be set aside because it appears to be too simple. Good ideas come in all shapes and sizes and are often not the big saving ideas.
- ❑ When an idea occurs, it should be written down as soon as possible.

Supervisors should be trained in suggestion scheme administration. The training should entail lectures, case studies, and group participation covering the following subjects:

- ❑ How to be successful in getting quality suggestions from subordinates.
- ❑ How to give support in the development and documenting of suggestions subordinates submit.
- ❑ How to make a speedy and accurate evaluation of savings and costs of suggestions.
- ❑ How to estimate implementation costs, time scheduling, skill and equipment requirements.

Organisations that make use of training will find that they not only receive better suggestions, but there is also an increase in submissions.

7.13 An efficient costing system

To enable a fair evaluation of the suggestion, the organisation should have an efficient costing system particularly when the award is based on net saving, i.e. gross saving less implementation costs. An inefficient costing system can result in disputes, disagreements and dissatisfaction which are demotivating factors.

7.14 A suitable name for the programme

It is absolutely essential that the correct name is chosen or given to the programme. The following should be borne in mind when choosing a name for the scheme:

- It should not be linked to previous programmes, especially any which were unsuccessful;
- it should describe the aim of the scheme;
- it should be short and to the point;
- it should be easy to remember;
- it should be unique; and
- it should offer the opportunity for publicity and advertising.

In addition, extreme care should be taken with the name, particularly with the current trend to use acronyms.

8. THE MANAGEMENT OF SUGGESTION SCHEMES

The position which a suggestion scheme is allocated in the organisational structure often reflects management's attitude towards the scheme. If the scheme is regarded as important it will consequently be positioned on a fairly senior level in the organisation's hierarchy and vice versa.

A successful suggestion scheme should be run as an integral part of the organisation, i.e. a marketing department. *The management of the suggestion scheme can be defined as the process through which the person or persons responsible for human resources attempt to use the available factors of production in the most cost-effective way possible, with the object of generating a maximum number of ideas from the work force and to compensate them for their ideas.* It is an unending process of planning, organising, leading, co-ordination and control of the attempts of others to achieve certain aims.

8.1 Planning

The objectives which have been identified should form the central core of planning, viz. to encourage creative suggestions from employees, to improve employer/employee relationships, to strengthen the competitive ability of the organisation, to compensate employees for ideas, to maintain work loyalty and, finally, to reduce the gap between the organisational goals and the needs of the employees.

Whether the scheme is new or an established system, the basic principles of planning should be adhered to, i.e. the formulation of goals, the gathering of information, the analysis and interpretation of information, the arrival at a final decision and the formulation of action plans. This is commonly known as the P.D.C.A. cycle (plan, do, check and analyse).

The manager of the suggestion scheme is continually having to make decisions between alternatives. (Examples: Is a suggestion which has been submitted an original idea? Who first proposed the suggestion? What level of compensation should be given for that suggestion?) Planning forms an integral part of the decision-making process. The success of a scheme depends, to a large degree, on making the correct decision as this decision will affect the employees fundamentally. This is most relevant in cases of awards and recognition. Incorrect or poor decisions can lead to doubts or open antagonism on the part of suggestors which can have a negative effect on the scheme.

Suggestion scheme planning includes the entire planning spectrum, namely routine, short-term and total planning.

There are various aids which may be used to help in the planning process. The most important are, inter alia, the following:

The determination of aims and objectives

Aims and objectives are necessary because the degree of success of the programme can then be measured over a particular time period. The planning will as a result involve the attainment of objectives.

A suggestion scheme policy

A policy which outlines a course of action is necessary and serves as a decision-making guideline. It should also be made part and parcel of the organisational policy and procedures which direct the entire spectrum of organisational activities. If this is done, the scheme policy will reflect the philosophies and attitudes of senior management as well as other interested parties, such as trade unions. In view of the importance of the philosophy, it should always be in writing so that it can serve as an authority and a guide in the making of decisions.

Procedures and methods

A scheme's policy should outline procedures and methods which describe specific methods of dealing with certain problems and completing certain actions. Guides and manuals are helpful aids which will ensure that procedures and methods are followed uniformly.

Rules and regulations

The suggestion scheme rules and regulations specify certain instructions which must be complied with under various scenarios. This results in the suggestion scheme goals being achieved through plans laid down. Rules and regulations are thus the instrument through which the scheme can be guided and controlled.

Budgets

A budget is a plan, expressed in figures, of anticipated results. The quantified statement can thus be in financial terms or in physical units. The suggestion scheme budget sets previously determined goals that can be compared in the controlling process in order to determine deviations and thus what corrective steps are required.

Programmes

A programme provides a detailed outline of the steps to be taken in order to achieve a specified goal, those responsible for each step, a set order of the steps taken and a date on which every step should start and be completed. The programme can be used as a successful instrument when special campaigns are made, for example by holding a suggestion week.

The greater the number of instruments that are built into the planning process, the more order there will be. Greater control can only be to the advantage of the scheme.

8.2 Organising

Organising, as a management function, refers to the organising of activities and the distribution of resources, the allocation of duties, the authority and responsibilities to persons in leadership positions. This determines the relationships between personnel, which promotes efficiency within the organisation.

Organising a suggestion scheme takes place in three phases, namely:

- during the inception of the scheme;
- during the existence of the scheme; and
- while activities are being executed.

Organising during the inception of the scheme

During this phase, attention should be paid to the organisational structure of the suggestion scheme department.

A final decision must be made regarding the positioning of the suggestion scheme department within the overall organisational structure. Where the suggestion scheme department is not independent, but forms part of another department, that department should be re-organised to ensure the success of the activities of the new section.

During this phase, the duties and responsibilities of the various related functions must be set out, as well as the future functions and role which the scheme is to play.

Organising during the existence of the scheme

During this phase, structural changes and modifications which have become necessary over time are made. A dynamic system demands continual adaptation to changing circumstances.

Organising while activities are being completed

The day-to-day organising takes place during this phase. This involves the organising of activities in order to achieve the aims of the suggestion scheme over a given time period and in the long term.

The organisational structure of a suggestion scheme

Organisational structure is the framework within which this process takes place. The authority and responsibility of every post is outlined in this framework. However, it should be remembered that a strong organisational structure does not necessarily guarantee good performance, but a weak structure will invariably lead to poor performance, no matter how strong individual management is.

As mentioned above, the suggestion scheme is usually implemented by the personnel department or by the industrial engineering department, however, there is a distinct advantage to be gained by not making the scheme a part of the personnel or labour relations departments as both of these departments are primarily advisory in nature.

The administration of the scheme by the industrial engineering department can be advantageous as this department is frequently involved in improving productivity, which is the cornerstone of the suggestion scheme. Furthermore, this department is not only familiar with the organisational aspects of the organisation, but also has the technical knowledge and experience which is essential for the successful running of such a scheme.

What is important is that responsibility for the suggestion scheme should be assigned to a member of senior management. Such a person is in a better position to gain the full co-operation and support of all the organisation's departments because of the position and authority he holds.

As far as the organisation is concerned, the following aspects related to the suggestion scheme should also be taken into account.

A centralised or a decentralised department

The size of the suggestion scheme department should be determined by the size of the organisation, the degree to which the operations are decentralised and the degree to which the various departments are geographically dispersed. In large, decentralised organisations where the various departments are geographically dispersed, it would be advisable to have a suggestion scheme co-ordinator at each unit, except for the centralised unit at the head office.

A centralised unit that co-ordinates the entire organisation's suggestion scheme has the following advantages:

- Advantages related to the implementation of suggestions are not confined to the unit where the suggestion was applied. Good suggestions can be applied throughout the organisation wherever possible.
- A uniform method of evaluation applies throughout the organisation, no matter how dispersed it is geographically.
- A uniform award system applies irrespective of the size of the unit in which the suggestor works.

The task of the suggestion scheme department

The general tasks of the suggestion scheme department are as follows:

- It should serve as a storage facility for all suggestions that are sent in.
- It should serve as an administrative office from where the scheme is not only managed but where the final administration takes place, such as the final evaluation and determination of award.

- It should handle all enquiries, complaints and appeals relating to suggestions and the scheme.
- It should ensure good communication with regard to the suggestion scheme through the available communication channels.
- It should ensure that neither the organisation nor the employee is exploited, but rather that both are treated fairly with regard to the sharing of benefits resulting from suggestions.

The manager or co-ordinator

It has previously been mentioned that relatively few personnel need be directly involved in the management of the scheme, but those that do manage it should be of high quality.

Possibly the most important person is the manager of the scheme, who should also be in charge of the suggestion scheme department. This is important because the success of the scheme relies heavily on this person. The higher the quality of the person directing the programme, the better will be the results achieved.

The ideal person in this position will normally be able to implement with considerable success nearly all the plans, while a poor appointment will often result in dismal failure. The title of the job is left to the discretion of the organisation. Some examples of titles that have been used are suggestion scheme manager, co-ordinator, suggestions director, chairman of the suggestion scheme, secretary and suggestion administrator.

Whenever there is a deterioration in the scheme, the first area to be examined is the manager of the scheme. With few exceptions it will be found that suggestion scheme work forms a small part of another manager's task or that the manager is an official who has reached the end of his career and is no longer interested in the work, or that it is a manager who does not fit in elsewhere in the organisation as a result of, for example, personality conflicts. The manager of the scheme should be chosen with great care and discretion. It is a very significant post which demands numerous qualities and it would be a grave error to appoint a good clerk to the position and then expect good results. Ideally he should be a full-time official with authority and who enjoys the full support of senior management. He should have knowledge of the business of his company, with broad experience of the organisation, and he should have faith in the working of the organisation and its policies. He should be capable of proper planning, organising, leading and controlling. He should be full of imagination and creativity, and he needs to be a *'salesman'* who is capable of developing an enthusiastic work force.

It is obvious that exceptionally high demands are placed on the person who takes up this post. This description is consistent with the features of the industrial engineer's post, which is why schemes are so often becoming the responsibility of the industrial engineering department. It should also be accepted that such personnel are scarce, with a high market value, which limits the availability of such people.

The suggestion committee

In most successful suggestion schemes the manager or co-ordinator is supported by the necessary assistants and a suggestion committee consisting of five to seven members representing the main functions of the organisation.

The members of this committee should be selected with the utmost care. Although some organisations select members who are not involved in management, it is generally found that the preferential choice is to elect people from management ranks.

The committee members can be appointed by senior management to:

- serve on a permanent basis, or
- serve on a temporary or rotational basis.

The advantage of the former is that there will be continuity because membership will only cease on the member's retirement, through death or through the decision of senior management. A further advantage is that all suggestions will always be evaluated in the same manner while the committee remains in existence.

The second alternative also has advantages, namely the possibility that committee norms which have become stale will be reduced with the periodic rotation of members resulting in new approaches and insights.

The suggestion committee is basically the policy-making body which also has the following responsibilities:

- To rule on the eligibility of suggestions whenever doubts arise.
- To assist in promotional and publicity programmes.
- To judge and evaluate suggestions for awards.
- To act as advisors to the suggestion scheme staff.
- To recommend improvements for the scheme.

In cases where a committee system is not used, the manager of the scheme should be able to canvas interested parties to evaluate suggestions. Proponents of this system of suggestion evaluation maintain that the problem with the committee system is convening regular meetings in the midst of busy schedules.

In cases where the organisation is decentralised and geographically dispersed, each branch should have a local committee to evaluate its own suggestions. They then make a recommendation to the central committee who will take the matter further.

In the committee system, the suggestion manager acts as the secretary, although in some organisations he serves as committee chairman. The role of chairman should be undertaken by a member of the management team.

8.3 Leading or directing

Leading is the means by which management guides people to work together voluntarily in completing tasks in order to achieve as efficiently as possible, the organisational objectives. Leadership is a vital part of the management process — the nucleus — because it supports the activities of the organisation and maintains the pursuit of goals. The prime concerns are the availability of information, the communication thereof, briefing where necessary, the implementation and supervision of plans. All these elements contribute greatly to the success of a suggestion scheme.

Whenever the most important requirements for effective leadership are analysed, their relevance to the success of the suggestion scheme becomes all the more evident.

The requirements are as follows:

Self orientation and motivation

The suggestion scheme manager should be familiar with the objectives and policies of the suggestion scheme. A clear long-term plan should have been prepared as well as the strategies to be employed in order to achieve these objectives. Apart from being self-motivated, he should be able to motivate the work force to come forward voluntarily with creative suggestions and ideas. A positive attitude towards the scheme is one of the prerequisites for a successful scheme. The enthusiasm and conviction of the manager or co-ordinator can play a decisive role in this regard.

Clear and concise instructions and communications

Effective communication and efficient communication channels are indispensable to a successful suggestion scheme. If suggestors are not speedily informed that their suggestions have been received and are being evaluated, the scheme will soon be regarded with suspicion.

When the scheme manager issues instructions, particular attention should be paid to the nature of the order, the method of conveying the instruction and the correct reception and interpretation of that instruction. This applies especially where suggestions are not accepted or where an award is made known. It may well be that the suggestor had high expectations of his suggestions, which did not materialise.

Guidance and information

The availability of information regarding the suggestion scheme is essential for its success. Employees in general, particularly the newcomers, should receive information regularly about the scheme as a whole, how to go about submitting a suggestion, what the awards will be, how they are calculated, and whose suggestions were successful. This kind of information will not only keep the personnel informed but will also have a motivational effect, especially where success stories are reported.

During the induction phase, employees should be made aware of the who, what, where, when and why of the scheme.

Control over the implementation of instructions

The manager of the suggestion scheme must ensure that system administrative instructions are carried out according to the schedule. For instance, suggestors should receive acknowledgement within five working days after a suggestion has been submitted.

Supervisory function

An instruction remains in force and must be executed until such time as:

- the task is completed to the satisfaction of the manager; or
- the instruction is withdrawn or recalled by the manager (or instructor).

Until either one of these phases is reached the task should be carried out continuously. It remains the manager's duty to ensure that the activities required to complete the task do not cease. If, for example it is decided that 10 % of the year's net savings should be paid out as a bonus to a suggestor, it is the manager's duty to see that this is done until top management decides otherwise.

The scheme manager should always be on the lookout for factors that will inhibit co-ordination and apply his abilities (i.e. his knowledge, skills and expertise) to remove these obstructions.

Mutual co-operation to achieve objectives

The basis for suggestion scheme success is the co-operation of the labour force. This co-operation should be voluntary for it to be of any use. The suggestion scheme manager should use all the means at his disposal to obtain the goodwill and co-operation of the workforce. Good leadership, effective communication, motivation, discipline, joint decision-making, co-ordinating practices and sound labour relations should be applied.

Leading always remains a difficult and strenuous task which takes up most of the manager's time. Unfortunately it is a task which cannot be avoided.

8.4 Co-ordination

Co-ordination within the realms of the suggestion scheme can be defined as a conscious effort on the part of the suggestion scheme manager to harmonise and co-ordinate the suggestions submitted by the various individuals and departments so that there is total co-operation in the achievement of the aims of the suggestion scheme, viz. stimulating the creative thought-processes of the employees, which in turn will lead to increased productivity.

The suggestion scheme manager and his personnel should keep the following in mind:

- Using the basic aims of the suggestion scheme, plans for the various departments should be co-ordinated to achieve the objectives. Targets of, say, two suggestions per month per department for a specific month should be set as an organisational goal. The departmental objectives must be co-ordinated with the objective in mind.
- The departments should be kept up to date with information regarding all aspects of the suggestion scheme. Furthermore, employees should be able to submit their suggestions to the suggestion scheme manager without any red tape, or to contact him should they have any queries. An efficiently

organised communication and information system is essential for good co-ordination of a suggestion scheme.

- Discussions between suggestion scheme personnel, departmental heads and the employees of the various departments should take place on a regular basis. The departmental heads should see themselves as part of the suggestion scheme and this can happen only if ideas and thoughts are exchanged continually. Problems which should receive attention during these discussions are, inter alia: How to increase the flow of suggestions, how to shorten time lapse between the submission of a suggestion and its acknowledgement, and how to overcome employee resistance to the scheme.
- Personal contact with departmental heads and employees should take place on a regular basis. The personal interest shown in employees will act as a motivator and contributes to better co-operation.

By applying these four factors, the co-ordination role of the scheme manager will be enhanced.

8.5 Controlling

Control is the measurement of activities, comparing them with set plans, and taking corrective actions, whenever deviations occur, or at times, the adjustment and updating of plans where fixed changes may occur. Control is the method by which the operation of the suggestion scheme plans and procedures are managed to ensure that the activities performed accord with the goals of the organisation.

It must be borne in mind that the management of a suggestion scheme, as with management in general, relies heavily on the existence of an effective communication and information system.

Control requires observation, comparison, measurement, evaluation and corrective action whenever deviations occur. This action may consist of modifying the plans or taking corrective steps.

The suggestion scheme is extremely sensitive to certain influences which may result in certain goals not being achieved. It is, therefore, necessary that there should be some form of control.

9. OBSTACLES IN THE WAY OF SUCCESSFUL SUGGESTION SYSTEMS

Together with the requirements for the successful implementation are obstacles that prevent suggestion systems from being successful. These obstacles have to be removed before the task of implementing the scheme can be addressed. They are:

9.1 Fear of the negative impact of suggestions

Every employee has the inherent fear that he will eventually work himself out of a job by submitting suggestions, particularly when they concern labour-saving ideas. Unless the idea is submitted by the group who should all benefit from the suggestion, the individual suggestor becomes unpopular. The rejection problem of the individual is worsened by the fact that he was compensated for his idea.

The rejection and isolation fears result in the development of a group mentality which discourages group members (that is, employees) from submitting suggestions.

One of the prerequisites for success of a suggestion scheme is the desire of management to make it successful. A cornerstone of trust is management's assurance that no one will lose his job as the result of a suggestion, whether in the short or the long term. Whenever labour-saving suggestions are made, the employees affected should be transferred to other departments or sections where they may become more productive.

When it becomes evident that management does not discharge people as a result of suggestions, the employees will not only have the desire to submit suggestions, but the group will also become less antagonistic towards the suggestor because the fear of being fired as a result of the suggestion has been eliminated.

Therefore, mutual co-operation between management and personnel is necessary to foster a healthy attitude towards the suggestion scheme and its general acceptance right from the start. Therefore, participation, two-way communication, explanation of the benefits for the employee, and for the organisation as a whole, are but a few of the aspects of a suggestion scheme.

9.2 Group resistance to individual compensation

A feeling of resentment may result among group members because compensation takes place on an individual basis. The opinion is that, especially at this level, most ideas result directly or indirectly from group discussions or discussions between individual group members, usually over a long period. The person who takes the initiative and submits the idea as his own suggestion and receives compensation is labelled an *idea thief* by the group. The suggestor is then branded and rejected by the group.

When management regards a suggestion received as one which has been submitted by the group to which the individual suggestor belongs, both the group and the individual benefit from this action. The former directly and the latter indirectly. The group is therefore the major player and receives the acknowledgement. This management action satisfies man's inherent need to belong. Instead of being negative, the group encourages its members to submit suggestions. Although it is the individual who produces the ideas, the group will assist in refining and making the ideas feasible, and it becomes a team effort to make it a practical issue. When it comes to the question of compensation, the group and not the individual must receive the award. The distribution of the compensation should be left to the group itself and they should decide on how the award will be distributed. Since the entire group benefits from the acknowledgement and financial reward, group resistance to individual compensation will be converted into group encouragement.

The element of competition can be introduced by setting savings goals for the various groups. This will motivate groups to generate more suggestions and ideas. In addition to the above, these actions result in more indirect benefits for management, viz.:

- Willingness of workers (the group members) to accept technological changes and to apply new methods and procedures successfully.
- Willingness of group members to help one another and to share their knowledge of shortcuts — a characteristic of a sound team spirit.

9.3 Writing out of suggestions

Many employees are not able to convey their thoughts in writing with clarity, but given the opportunity to demonstrate and to express themselves orally do so with considerable success. However, with a traditional type of suggestion scheme this cannot be easily accommodated. This type of communication usually takes place after the suggestion has gone through the first phase of evaluation. If the suggestion has merit but the evaluators have some doubts, the suggestor may be asked to elucidate his ideas to remove uncertainty. Because of the pressures of work, suggestion scheme administrators may decline suggestions in the first phase because of these uncertainties.

The suggestor is not left to his own devices to record the suggestion in writing since the fear of idea theft is no longer evident. Since it now becomes a team effort the suggestion is written down fully and logically. Group members may ask similar questions and look for explanations, thereby simulating the suggestion administrator's actions during the initial evaluation phase. This group interaction helps to solve problems which are usually the downfall of many suggestions during this crucial first phase of evaluation.

9.4 Resistance by the supervisor

Because of the suggestion scheme design, many suggestions find their way directly to the administrator or via the suggestion box and thereby bypassing the supervisor. In both cases, the supervisor remains oblivious to the fact that a suggestion has been submitted and registered. Many suggestions concern the shortcomings of the supervisor himself or problems which he should have known about. Supervisors, therefore, often view suggestion schemes as a threat to their future. They therefore oppose them and may unconsciously sabotage them or even ignore their existence.

In those companies where suggestions are channelled through the supervisor, it can happen that good suggestions are eliminated because the supervisor regards them as impracticle and as a result of this attitude, employees may fear that they will be discriminated against if the suggestion is accepted. The natural reaction is to avoid friction and possible reprisals by not submitting suggestions. These ideas or suggestions are therefore shelved and never see the light of day.

A group usually consists of a supervisor and his team, and since the supervisor forms part of the group, he shares in the recognition and compensation which the group may receive. Although the idea may come from an individual, the supervisor feels that he is part of the group and is not being bypassed or threatened. As a group member and leader of the group, he experiences the whole development of the idea.

The supervisor's participation in the process changes his outlook toward suggestions. He no longer sees them as a threat but rather as a tool for solving problems in his area and for which both he and his team receive recognition and compensation. The team effort enhances his image instead of breaking it down. As a result the supervisor becomes an active role player by agreeing to and supporting (and in many cases helping to improve) suggestions with wise advice. The fear of discrimination and recriminations fades and employees come to the conclusion that it is a team effort and the supervisor is an integral part of that team.

As a result of this interaction the relationship between the supervisor and his subordinates undergoes a vast improvement, a change which benefits the entire organisation.

In addition, the supervisor will actively encourage his subordinates to find new ideas, which develops a tightly knit group with a strong identity.

Another important aspect to be borne in mind, is that active groups which participate regularly become more adept at making decisions on the proposals of group members.

9.5 Trade Union resistance

Because of the upward communication channel function performed by suggestion schemes, they meet with resentment and resistance from the unions, who regard that function as one of their rightful duties. Unions also tend to have an influence whenever any improvements in work methods are considered.

The fear that traditional suggestion schemes will result in headcount and bonus reductions is usually the true reason for resistance from unions and their leaders.

Employee improvement in participative management and in the affairs of the organisation is essential and this may well mean that management must co-operate fully with the trade unions. They cannot be ignored.

In participative management there is often a tendency for groups who experience problems to solve them without resorting to union help.

We must reiterate that management must give employees the assurance that suggestions will not cause any redundancies. This assurance will allay union fears that members who make suggestions will lose their jobs.

The upward communication function which is viewed by the unions as their prerogative primarily because of the fear that their members and themselves may be disadvantaged by any upward flow of information. The 'no-retrenchment' assurance should eliminate this fear.

Whenever production bonuses are lost or discontinued they can be replaced by the suggestion award which is paid to the group instead of the individual. When the focus of the individual, the group or the union is on productivity improvements, a common goal exists and conflicting management bodies will not develop.

The co-operation of a union and its leaders is essential in eliminating resistance to suggestion schemes. The advantages to be gained by the employees by participating in suggestion schemes must be emphasised. The co-operation of the union, particularly during the stage when union activities gain prominence, is absolutely essential and could possibly make the difference between success and failure.

10. IMPLEMENTATION OPTIONS OF A SUGGESTION SCHEME

On implementation of a suggestion scheme the organisation has three options which it may exercise, viz.:

- Use of a consultant service to research, design and eventually implement the suggestion scheme (sometimes also undertaking the administration).
- By adopting systems which are in use at other organisations.
- By conducting its own research, designing, developing and implementing its own system.

Each option has both positive and negative aspects which management must evaluate before deciding on the method to adopt.

A few of the advantages and disadvantages are presented below:

Advantages of using a consultant for implementation

- Consultants who make themselves available for this type of work are usually knowledgeable about the latest developments, both locally and abroad.
- Because the consultant is independent of the organisation, personnel will not have to be taken away from their normal

functions in order to undertake the project. This advantage becomes even more attractive where the consultant also takes care of the administration, particularly since the organisation does not need to allocate headcount to the task.

- Because the consultant is familiar with the latest developments, the pilot study and development of the system are completed relatively quickly. The implementation of the system is speeded up and the lead time between announcement and implementation of the system is reduced. There is insufficient time for resistance to build up because the results and advantages become evident to the employee within a very short time.
- As an outsider, the consultant's ideas will probably be more acceptable to the employees than those of colleagues. The orientation process will be facilitated, especially where the consultant succeeds in gaining the confidence of the employees.

Possible disadvantages if a consultant does the implementation

- Before a consultant can implement a productivity improvement programme with any degree of success, he needs to familiarise himself with the organisation and its personnel. However, the time available for the familiarisation process is severely restricted (in order to gain an advantage for a speedy implementation) and there is considerable doubt as to whether he will succeed. It takes a relatively long time to analyse complex human beings. If the study is poorly executed it may result in an unacceptable system which is rejected and resisted by the employees.
- Being an outsider the consultant may be regarded with suspicion by the employees. He may be perceived as a stranger who has no empathy for their situation and the inherent problems. The fact that the consultant is not a member of the employee group may result in resistance and rejection.
- The consultant is a professional person who usually commands a high fee, considerably more than some of the organi-

sation's employees, resulting in the establishment and implementation of the suggestion scheme relatively expensive.

Advantages of adopting an existing system.

One of the most important advantages of adopting an existing system is that most of the teething problems with the system have already been resolved by the developer. Whenever an existing system is used the management of the organisation which plans to use it should make sure that the system is modified to suit their requirements. Obviously, there is an added advantage if it can be used as is or with one or two minor adaptations. The following two advantages will result, namely:

- ❑ It will be relatively cheap as very few adaptations are required, resulting in little or no development cost.
- ❑ The system can be implemented relatively quickly and the employees become aware of the results soon.

Possible disadvantages of adopting an existing system.

- ❑ It is very rarely possible to adopt a system from another organisation without making changes, no matter how small they are, because no two organisations are exactly alike. It could be that two organisations are identical but the external constraints (for example a different type of clients, difference in climate, geographical site, etc.).
- ❑ Although a successful organisation scheme requires a great deal of research and development, very few organisations are prepared to part with information on a no-charge basis especially if it is very successful. Research costs are high and one can expect that the asking price for a successful suggestion system recipe will be relatively high.

Advantages of a unique scheme

- ❑ A suggestion scheme that is developed by the organisation will be tailor-made to suite its own requirements.
- ❑ During the development phase, the administrators responsible for the suggestion system, will develop confidence in the

entire programme. This will enable them to administer the system with a great deal of confidence, especially in times of crises.

- The development process also forms part of the awareness phase involving the rest of the personnel because of their indirect involvement they actually become part of the information collection phase. When the system eventually goes *'live'*, the employees are well aware of the scheme.
- Another advantage of a unique scheme is that employees currently on the payroll are used for research, development, implementation and the maintenance of the system. No external flow of funds takes place and there are no external creditors.

Possible disadvantages of a unique system.

- The development of a unique scheme is nothing more than a research project which needs to be thoroughly executed. Because the process can be lengthy it rules out the changes of a speedy establishment.
- The initial costs of the system can be relatively high on account of the direct and indirect costs of the development phase.
- Regardless of the amount of research which has been undertaken, it is very seldom that implementation of a new system goes without a hitch. The value of the programme is often placed in doubt if problems are experienced with the evaluation of suggestions and the related compensation. The uncertainty among the employees leads to withdrawal from, and a resistance to the scheme. Trial runs must be undertaken by management with the greatest care. Even though it may be a trial run, it is often the most important phase of the implementation stage because first impressions are often the most lasting.

Regardless of the choice of method of implementation, there will always be costs involved, but these costs must be regarded as an investment. The method which is selected to establish and implement a suggestion scheme will determine the size of the investment.

11. THE FIVE PHASES IN SUGGESTION SCHEME IMPLEMENTATION

The successful implementation of a suggestion scheme depends on the phases outlined below in Figure 1.

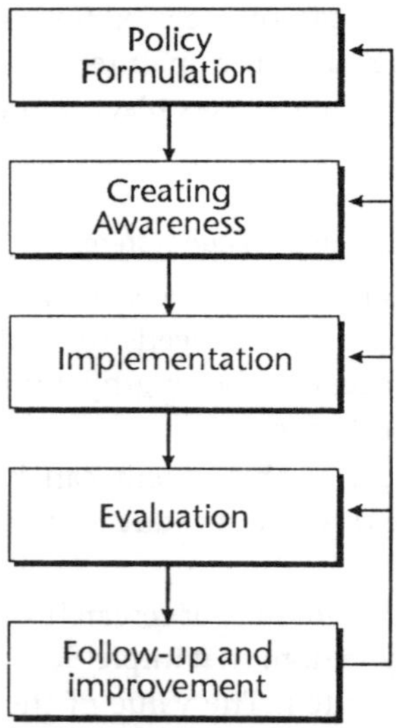

Figure 1
Phases of implementation of a suggestion scheme

11.1 The policy formulation phase

A policy is defined as a verbal or written guideline which defines the boundaries within which management will operate. Although the policy can be verbal, according to the definition above, it is preferable to have it in writing. This eliminates the possibility of ambiguity and misconstruction. A written policy can be communicated more efficiently and every employee will know what they can expect from the scheme.

If it were possible to compile a policy which took care of every eventuality, the result would be something akin to a statute book. This defeats the object of having a policy document which contains the essential rules and is used as a frame of reference only.

A suggestion scheme policy should contain at least all of the following:

- ❑ The aims of the scheme;
- ❑ A definition of a suggestion or idea;
- ❑ Categories or types of suggestions that do not necessarily qualify for the scheme;
- ❑ The composition and tasks of the suggestion committee;
- ❑ Who will oversee the administration of the scheme;
- ❑ Employees who are excluded from participation;
- ❑ Compensation for ideas;
- ❑ The actions to be taken when an idea is already under consideration;
- ❑ The procedure to be followed when suggestions are declined;
- ❑ The procedure to be followed when declined suggestions are re-evaluated;
- ❑ Anonymous suggestions — to what extent will they be allowed;
- ❑ The responsibilities and lawful aspects with regard to:
  - — the cessation of ownership rights;
  - — the suggestions of non-employees;
  - — finality in decision-making;
  - — patentable ideas; and
  - — costs incurred.

Annexure 1 is a conceptual policy document which may be used by management as a guideline.

11.2 The creating awareness phase

Once a policy has been formulated the suggestion scheme awareness phase begins. During the introduction stage of the scheme the awareness phase assumes a very important role. Interest and awareness are of prime importance regardless of how well the scheme is supported and patronised. It has to be sold just as with any other goods or services constantly calling for new techniques and publicity. Success stories play an important role in scheme publicity.

The aim of an on-going awareness programme is threefold:

- To communicate information such as objectives, methods, advantages and the policy of the suggestion scheme to the employees.
- To develop and maintain co-operation and confidence in the scheme, especially when the programme has already been implemented; and
- To stimulate interest and participation in creative processes which are focused on improvement.

During the publicity and the continual awareness creating programme (Annexure 2) the following techniques and aids may be used:

- brochures;
- posters;
- audiovisual material;
- circulars;
- publications in the inhouse newspapers or news letters;
- notices;
- exhibitions; and
- competitions.

The awareness phase is extremely important and the influence which it has on the suggestion scheme success must not be underestimated.

11.3 The implementation phase

Until the policy and administration details have been finalised, a suggestion scheme cannot be implemented successfully.

The awareness phase will have created an air of expectancy among the employees and these expectations have to be met if success is to be achieved.

After the starting date of the suggestion programme is made known, employees will still be hesitant and apprehensive about participating. This has been ascribed to the fact that the employees stand back to see how another employee's suggestion is handled. It could be quite some time before this reticence is broken. The role of the supervisor becomes vitally important at this stage. The spontaneous encouragement, help and support of the supervisor is essential.

Three techniques may be used to break down the silent stumbling block. The first technique involves giving a small sum of money, say R5, or a gift, for example a set of cuff links or an exclusive key-ring, or something else of value to *each* person who submits a suggestion during a given time period. This may result in a number of worthless suggestions being submitted merely for the prizes, but the campaign will, nevertheless, yield a number of worthwhile suggestions, the savings of which often cover the cost of the promotion. An informative campaign to explain thoroughly the workings of the system could help dispel any initial fears. A similar type of programme could be used to elicit suggestions covering a particular topic, e.g. safety.

The second alternative is to set participation-level goals for the supervisors and their subordinates. A common method is to establish the previous levels attained and increase the goal by one or two suggestions for the next period. An improvement in the quality of the suggestions being submitted can also be used as an objective. Monetary savings are also used as effective goal setting, e.g. where the previous net saving resulting from a suggestion was, say, R12 000 per annum, then the new objective would be an amount in excess of R12 000 for the following year.

These monetary-based goals may have a negative effect in that employees may look only for those suggestions which make large savings at the expense of the smaller saving suggestions. A large number of these small savings could, when added together, be greater than many big single savers. The big single saving suggestion may also never be implemented.

A third method of stimulating participation is to offer a cash bonus or recognition, based on the number of suggestions which were accepted during a specific time span. This award is over and above the normal system compensation. An example of this method is shown in Table 1 below. By following the guidelines in the table a suggestor who had seven accepted suggestions would receive R500 plus a R100 for every suggestion over the initial number of 5, i.e. 2 x R100. Total bonus is thus R700. Another who had 29 accepted suggestions would then receive R3 350 + R1 200 = R4 750

Table 1
CALCULATION OF PARTICIPATION BONUS

Number of accepted suggestions	Initial Award	Additional amount per suggestion, over and above the minimum in A
5 to 10	R500	R100
11 to 15	R1 000	R120
16 to 20	R1 600	R150
21 to 25	R2 350	R200
26 and over	R3 350	R300

These techniques may be applied in different ways in an attempt to shorten the resistance period. The longer this resistance continues, the longer it will take to determine the value of the programme.

Patience is a virtue and no more so than during the implementation phase. Time must be given for the system to become accepted and established as *'part of the business'* before any hasty evaluations are made.

11.4 The evaluation phase

When evaluating a productivity improvement programme, which is what a suggestion scheme is, five aspects must be considered to determine whether it is succeeding or deteriorating. These aspects are as follows:

- ❑ The perception which the employees and management have of the programme;
- ❑ the attitude displayed openly by management and employees toward the scheme;
- ❑ the support the scheme receives from the employees;
- ❑ the value the employees attach to the scheme; and
- ❑ the cost effectiveness of the scheme.

The *entire* labour force, which includes management, should be familiar with the existence of the scheme as well as the modus operandi. The publicity campaigns and awareness programmes have obviously not been as effective as they should have been if there are employees with no knowledge of the scheme. It may mean that there are other logistical problems, which were not initially identified, which need to be identified and resolved without delay.

The introduction of a suggestion scheme into an organisation implies that certain actions and reactions are expected from the employees as well as management. Examples are: suggestions are 'posted' in the suggestion box or handed to the co-ordinators, evaluation meetings take place; awards are calculated and presented on the appropriate occasions; suggestions are implemented. All these activities and the frequency with which they occur is indicative of the success of the programme.

When a suggestion scheme is introduced with senior management's support and approval, it is hardly likely that the entire work force will lend their support to the programme. If, during the first year, only 60 % support the programme and this figure rises to 70 % in the second year, it can be assumed that the programme is a success.

If there is a greater show of interest in the programme by an increase in participation or an influx of enquiries, it would be safe to assume with a large degree of certainty that the programme has gained in credibility and importance.

The cost-effectiveness of the programme is also an important yardstick in determining the programme's success. Because the suggestion scheme can be regarded as a mini-organisation in itself, with its own management and budgets, it is also expected to make a *profit*. A *profit* in this context means that benefits — monetary benefits as far as possible — should exceed the costs of the scheme over a given period of time. The costs in this case are the overall suggestion administrative costs plus the awards paid to employees for their suggestions over a given period of time.

If the benefits of the scheme are less than its costs over a period of time, a *loss* is being incurred and urgent attention has to be given to the scheme. Regardless of what the yardsticks are, it is important that the programme be evaluated from time to time. This will give the assurance that the programme is living up to expectations and achieving its objectives (refer to Annexures 4/1 for an evaluation questionaire and 4/2 for a monthly/yearly report form).

11.5 The follow-up and improvement phase

If the results emanating from the evaluation phase are not as good as anticipated, an investigation should be undertaken to examine the possible causes. It should determine whether the policy formulation was correct in the light of the experience gained through the operation of the programme, whether the awareness phase really achieved its intended objective, or whether the implementation phase was unsuccessful.

Owing to changing circumstances it is necessary that all levels of management re-affirm their commitment to and support for the programme.

Once the necessary improvements have been brought about the entire cycle starts from scratch, beginning with the awareness phase (refer Figure 1). Far from being a one-off exercise, it is an oft-repeated process. The reason is obvious — a suggestion scheme is a dynamic system and needs to adapt to meet changing circumstances.

12. THE SUBMISSION OF SUGGESTIONS

One of the prerequisites of a formal suggestion scheme is that suggestions must be in writing before being evaluated. They may be written on blank paper or submitted on a preprinted form (refer to annexure 1/2). Because the evaluation process is simplified by standardisation, the latter system is preferable. If all the relevant information is supplied on the form the evaluation process is speeded up. All unnecessary information is left off the form. An organisation which is considering a preprinted suggestion form should bear the following factors in mind:

- ❑ The form should be simple and easy to use. It should be remembered that employees with varying education levels will be using the same form.
- ❑ The form should provide sufficient space for all the required administration information such as surname, initials, job position, work area, telephone number, employee number and department. It should be presented in such a way so as to simplify the task of the suggestions office.
- ❑ The form should be designed so as to assist the suggestor to describe the current as well as the improved situation in order to facilitate the evaluation process.
- ❑ A summary of the most important rules and regulations should be printed on the reverse side of the form. This ensures that no ineligible suggestions are submitted since the suggestor is aware of what is acceptable.
- ❑ The form should be eye-catching, yet user-friendly.
- ❑ The form must be designed in such a way as to limit the suggestions to only one per form.

In order to retain objectivity during the evaluation process, the form can be designed in such a way so as to remove the personal details of the suggestor from the form once the suggestion number has been allocated.

The normal channels used when the physical submission takes place are usually directly to the responsible official, through the supervisor or via a suggestion box.

The suggestion boxes should be placed where they can be reached without too much effort, usually away from entrances or places where a lot of traffic is experienced. Placing them in out-of-the-way places may be courting disaster. Suggestion boxes may be unsuccessful for the following reasons.

- Management's greatest concern is that the employees may use the suggestions boxes primarily as a channel for complaints as opposed to a channel for constructive ideas. This may be because employees are unable to differentiate between a constructive suggestion and a complaint, or the fact that employees view the box as an ideal anonymous complaints channel.
- Many employees have problems in transferring their thoughts to paper and the resulting suggestion is often vague and ambiguous. The net result is that the suggestion scheme administrator cannot make head or tail of the suggestion and rejects it.
- Suggestions that are prematurely rejected can result in waning enthusiasm for the programme. When the enthusiasm falls, so does the level in the suggestion boxes.
- Suggestion boxes are inanimate. There is no human contactor and interpersonal exchanges of thoughts between employees and supervisors. The supervisor could develop a negative attitude towards suggestions channeled through the suggestion box as he is not consulted about these suggestions.
- Some managers and supervisors abdicate their responsibility of promoting and interacting with the employees to encourage participation because they believe the box is sufficient. A

suggestion box is merely a piece of furniture nailed to the wall, which, if left there long enough, will be treated as a piece of furniture and totally disregarded. If a determined effort is not made to encourage employees to participate and use the suggestion boxes, they will remain empty.

Written confirmation of receipt of a suggestion is necessary, not only to satisfy the suggestor, but also to establish a registration time and date, thereby facilitating administration. The registration time and date will avoid future questions as to which was first.

Receipt acknowledgement may be made in various forms, but should contain at least the following information:

- The suggestor's name and department;
- The allocated suggestion number;
- The topic of suggestion;
- The date and time when the suggestion was received; and
- A few words of thanks for the effort put in by the suggestor, and the hope that the suggestion will be successful.

A standard preprinted postcard or letter with appropriate spaces for relevant information can be used. If the cards or letters are too impersonal an impression of indifference may be conveyed. If it is at all possible, the cards and letters should be completed in matching type which lends just that bit of a personal touch. A nice touch would be a personal letter signed by the Chief Executive Officer. This would be appreciated by the employees and obviously have an enormous impact.

Organisations which have computer facilities can programme a suggestion scheme in such a way that whenever an idea is registered it automatically prints a personal acknowledgement or receipt.

Quite often identical suggestions are received within a short period. The problem arises of determining which was first. This can be overcome by date-stamping the suggestion on receipt and then recording the time of registration.

Computerising the suggestion system will simplify the administration process. If these facilities are not available manual registers must be maintained. A numerical register, a name register and a topic register should be maintained.

The NUMERICAL REGISTER simplifies the allocation of numbers to suggestions. Additional information such as registration time and date, the subject, the name of the suggestor, his position and the department in which he works should be recorded.

The NAME REGISTER serves as a follow-up register to determine which suggestions have not been evaluated. It should include the following details:

- suggestor;
- suggestion number;
- subject;
- whether the suggestion is accepted or declined;
- estimated first year savings resulting from the suggestion; and
- the amount of the award to the suggestor.

The SUBJECT REGISTER helps in determining if similar suggestions are currently in the system. The information in this register is usually in alphabetical order according to the subject or the details of the subject, plus other information such as the suggestion number, the date submitted and the date the suggestion was finalised.

On receipt of the suggestion, a number is allocated, and if the suggestion form is designed in a certain way, the suggestor's personal details can be omitted, thereby ensuring anonymity.

Confidentiality should be maintained when dealing with suggestions. This is done not only to protect the suggestor but also the organisation especially when a suggestion could benefit its opposition. (refer Annexure 3).

13. THE EVALUATION OF SUGGESTIONS

Objectivity, open-mindedness and fairness are the principles of sound evaluations. The initial view should be the assumption that all suggestions are beneficial until the evaluation proves otherwise.

The suggestion committee or specific persons appointed should be responsible for evaluating the suggestions. Ideally, suggestions should be evaluated on an ongoing basis but where this is impractical, particularly in small organisations with relatively few suggestions, the evaluations should be carried out periodically. It is essential that these evaluations are carried out on set dates which are not too far apart, e.g. weekly, fortnightly or even monthly.

Research has shown that there is a correlation between the participation level and the time taken to evaluate suggestions and providing feedback. The feedback time should be as short as possible, particularly where personal contact has been made with the suggestor.

The following guidelines will contribute to a regulated evaluation of suggestions:

- ❑ Where possible, start the evaluation by holding a discussion with the suggestor.
- ❑ Fill in the dates in which the different information is received on the evaluation form.
- ❑ Make sure that the suggestor was the originator of the idea and that it was his initiative. In other words, prevent idea theft.
- ❑ The evaluator(s) should maintain their objectivity and remain neutral.
- ❑ The evaluator should take care to eliminate personal bias.
- ❑ The evaluation should not be affected by the negative attitude of any other employee or supervisor until such time as the evaluation is finalised.
- ❑ The suggestor should not under any circumstances be rewarded until such time as it is confirmed that the suggestion can be applied.

Figure 2 represents the flow of suggestions in the evaluation process. Read this together with Annexure 4.

14. REJECTED SUGGESTIONS

According to research, approximately 75 % of all suggestions are declined and as a result the strategy of the suggestion scheme should cater for these eventualities.

Whenever a suggestion is declined it should be dealt with in such a way so as not to alienate the employees from the suggestion scheme. The suggestor should be given the full reasons why the suggestion was declined.

Suggestors should be thanked for their efforts and should be encouraged to continue supporting the scheme. Sometimes the personal contact with the suggestor indicates the interest in new ideas and has the added motivational effect. These contacts could perhaps lead to additional information about the idea which may change the whole perception of the suggestion.

Declined suggestions may be re-evaluated when:

- The suggestor appeals, in other words he believes that the suggestion has not been adequately evaluated. Suggestors do become very frustrated when their ideas are declined, but they should be given the opportunity to state their case personally in order to supplement the information on their suggestion form.
- Circumstances may have changed which could result in a previously declined suggestion becoming feasible.
- A suggestion is declined during the initial evaluation. The idea may have definite merit but due to various constraints cannot be implemented at that specific stage.

Although rejected suggestions poses a threat to the success of the scheme, it could have the reverse effect of actually stimulating participation provided it is handled correctly. Participation is indicative of the employees' interest and shows that they are able to think constructively about the problems. In spite of a suggestion being declined, the organisation should acknowledge and recognise the interest and thought which the employee has put into the idea. The objective of the rejection notice should be

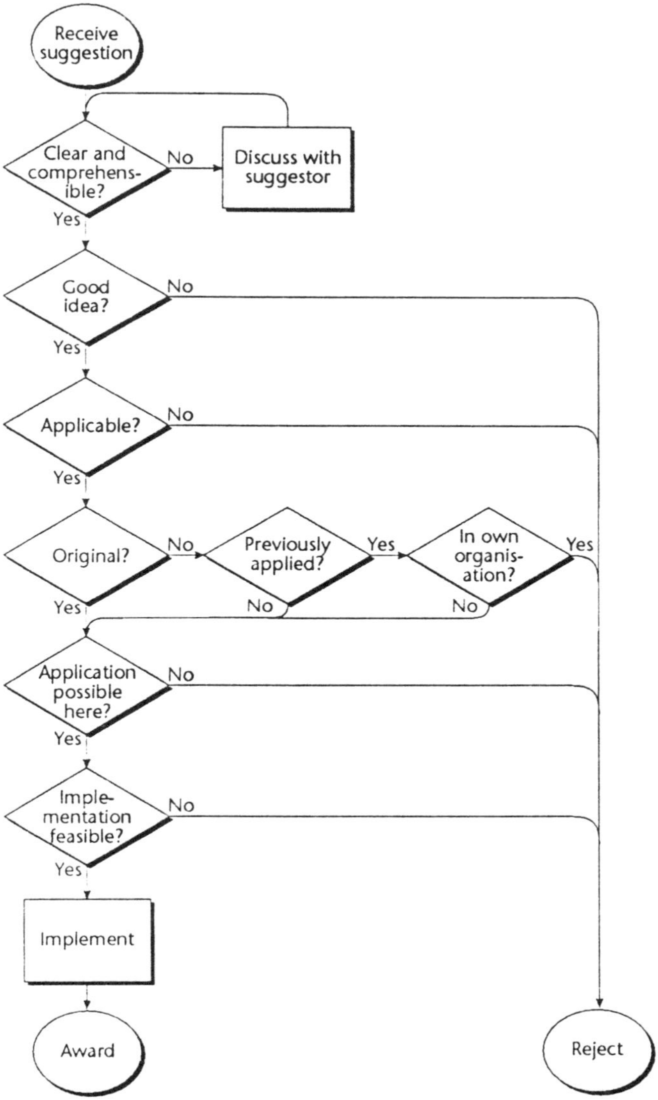

Figure 2

A flow diagram of suggestions in the evaluation process

twofold, firstly, to thank the employee and advise him of the reason why it was declined and, secondly, to encourage him to become more creative.

15. PATENTS

Research has indicated that relatively few patentable ideas originate from suggestion schemes.

In most organisations which operate suggestion schemes the tendency is to reward suggestors financially for successful ideas. If a suggestion does appear to have potential and could revolutionise a process, the suggestion committee or the responsible department, who would evaluate the suggestion, should investigate the possibility of patenting the idea. This could be undertaken by the organisation's legal advisor or by patent attorneys. The costs involved would be recovered by the patent and savings generated. If the organisation bears the cost of patenting the idea, it could motivate employees to look for patentable ideas at no cost to themselves.

Most organisations have a clause in their employment policy which covers the eventuality of an employee coming up with a patentable idea. It becomes the property of the organisation but some agreement is usually reached between the two parties since the idea could be used by outsiders. The aspects of patents should be covered in the scheme policy. The following is a typical example of a clause which should be included in the suggestion scheme policy:

> Suggestions, which in the opinion and at the discretion of the suggestion committee, can be patented, will be referred to the relevant authorities for patent evaluation for patent rights without the necessary consent of the suggestor who will also not bear any costs involved. Should the patent be registered, it will be done in the name of the organisation and the suggestor. Fifty per cent (50 %) of the royalties resulting from the patent will be paid to the suggestor within thirty (30) days of receipt of such royalties.

If a suggestion which results in changes to machinery, equipment or tooling is received, accepted and implemented, the onus is on the organisation to reward the suggestor. There is no responsibility on the supplier or manufacturer of the equipment to become involved. The organisation could consider passing the idea on to the supplier or manufacturer who may, if they so wish, consider a further reward to the suggestor.

It would appear to be a generally accepted practice that organisations which have research and development departments exclude these personnel from participating even though the idea could be patented, the view being that they were appointed and paid for their creative skills.

16. SUGGESTION AWARDS*

Although compensation is not a prerequisite of a formal suggestion scheme, it is generally recognised that financial awards are a prime reason for a successful scheme. The award should bear some relationship to circumstances of the suggestion as well as the amount of effort on the part of the suggestor.

One aspect of awards which is often ignored and yet is vitally important is the formula used to calculate the award amount. It should be simple and easily understood by the employees. Complicated formulae raise suspicions that the employer is not being entirely honest as far as the reward is concerned. This is definitely an area where the simplicity principle applies so that everybody understands how the amounts are calculated.

Awards are not won by employees when submitting suggestions, instead they are earned by initiative, innovation and creativity. It is remuneration for additional effort which is a very good reason why the award system should be adequate.

In order to achieve the desired results — employee participation — an award system should meet the following criteria:

- The employee should be aware of the existence of an award system;

* Also refer to Annexure 4.

- The employee should be familiar with the requirements to enable him to earn an award;
- The employee should be eligible to receive an award;
- There must be a direct relationship between the award and the performance which is being rewarded; and
- All evaluations should be fair and unbiased.

Criteria should be laid down for the award aspect of the suggestion scheme. In addition the award should be coupled to the suggestion and should relate to the specific circumstances and the amount of effort the suggestor put into formulating the suggestion.

Savings on benefits from suggestions fall into two categories, calculable, tangible savings/benefits and incalculable , intangible savings/benefits. The savings of the former are relatively easy to calculate and can be expressed in monetary terms. Incalculable or intangible savings tend to be subjective and cannot be measured.

16.1 Awards for tangible savings

There are four basic methods of calculating the award amounts, viz.:

- the amount is based on a fixed percentage of the saving;
- the use of a points system;
- the use of formulae; and
- the use of a table.

16.1.1 The fixed percentage method

The fixed percentage method also has a number of variations when it comes to reward calculations. Usually it is calculated on the saving (net or gross). Certain variations in the method are as follows:

- A fixed percentage (for example 10 %) of the first year's net savings with no ceiling;
- A fixed percentage (for example 10 %) of the first year's net savings with a specific maximum (for example R10 000); and

- A fixed percentage (for example 5 %) of the first year's net saving with a reduced fixed percentage (for example 2,5 %) on the second year's net saving.

The advantage of this type of calculation is that it is relatively easy and simple to understand.

16.1.2 The points method

The suggestion value is determined with the aid of a table which has been drawn up for that specific purpose. Points are allocated to factors such as savings, the merits of the suggestion and the overall improvements which will result from the suggestion based on a predetermined scale.

The current value per point should be agreed upon and should be valid for a specific length of time.

The total points score is multiplied by the rate per point to determine the reward amount. Table 2 is an example of a tariff table.

16.1.3 The formula method

The reward calculation using formulae can be made in a number of ways. It ranges from a relatively simple method to one which is highly technical in nature and most complicated. The rationale behind the use of a formula is that certain factors play a role and must be taken into account.

These factors can be weighted, which may be either to the suggestor's advantage or his disadvantage. Table 3 illustrates this point.

When the weighting is to the disadvantage of the suggestor it becomes very unpopular with employees as they feel they are being discriminated against.

16.1.3 The tabular method

The reward is determined primarily by *two factors* in the table, namely the frequency with which the suggestion will be used and the present condition (Table 4).

Table 2
A TARIFF TABLE FOR TANGIBLE SUGGESTIONS

DATE: . . . . NUMBER OF SUGGESTOR OR EMPLOYEE:. . . . .

NUMBER:. . . . .

Criteria	Basis of points awarded	Points	Points awarded
1. *Saving* Award points for tangible or intangible saving as a result of a suggestion that leads to a reduction in cost or an increase in production.	Small saving Significant saving Large saving	1–7 8–16 17–25	
2. *The merit of the suggestion* The degree of ingenuity, initiative, effort, technical knowledge and use of time.	Minimal Significant Large saving	1–6 7–13	
3. *Overall improvement as a result of the suggestion* For aspects that are not included in 1 and 2 above, e.g. improved working working relations, organisational image, employee relations in working conditions.	Specify	1–5	
Total points			

Total awarded in rands: . . . . points × R . . . . = R . . . .

Note:
- Where the criterium does not apply, score 0.
- R . . . . . is awarded for every point.

Signed: . . . .
(CHAIRMAN)

Table 3
TWO EXAMPLES OF AWARD CALCULATION USING A FORMULA

Suggestion award: Tangible savings
DATE: . . . . .NAME AND NUMBER OF SUGGESTOR. . . . .

Criteria	Example One	Example Two
A. THE TASK		
1. The suggestion is part of the proposer's task.	0,0	0,0
2. The suggestion occasionally forms part of the suggestor's task.	0,5	0,6
3. The suggestion does not form part of the suggestor's task at all.	1,0	0,9
B. KNOWLEDGE OF THE AREA		
1. The organisation is aware of the idea but has not used it.	0,0	0,0
2. The suggestion is known and is used in another work area.	0,5	0,3
3. The suggestion is known, but is seldom used in the organisation.	0,75	0,6
4. The suggestion is completely new and original for the task.	1,0	0,9
C. DESCRIPTION OF THE SUGGESTION		
1. The suggestion is nothing more than a statement.	0,9	0,3
2. The suggestion is vague.	1,0	0,6
3. The suggestion is explicit.	1,1	1,0
D. THE ORGANISATION'S CONTRIBUTION TOWARDS THE SUCCESS OF THE SUGGESTION		
1. A significant contribution.	0,4	0,1
2. A reasonable contribution.	0,6	0,3
3. A minor contribution.	0,8	0,6
4. Minimal or no contribution.	1,0	0,9

E. SIGNIFICANCE OF THE SUGGESTION		
1. The suggestion affects production as a whole.	0,8	0,7
2. The suggestion affects a number of production lines.	0,9	0,8
3. The suggestion affects a few production lines.	1,0	0,9
4. The suggestion affects a single production line.	1,1	1,0
F. WORKER LEVEL		
1. The suggestor is a normal employee.	1,0	1,0
2. The suggestor is a low level supervisor.	0,8	0,8
3. The suggestor is part of middle management.	0,6	0,6
4. The suggestor is part of top management.	0,4	0,4
G. THE NATURE OF THE SUGGESTION		
1. The suggestion is simple and obvious.	0,5	0,2
2. The suggestion is simple/plain but requires closer examination.	0,5	0,2
3. The suggestion is revolutionary (unique) in nature.	1,5	1,0

. . . percentage saving serves as a basis for the value of the compensation.

Compensation:
(. . . per cent of savings) × A × B × C × D × E × F × G

Example 1: Maximum value is 1,815 × (. . . per cent of saving)
Example 2: Maximum value is 0,271 × (. . . per cent of saving)

The usage frequency factors indicate the number of times that a suggestion is used within a particular time frame. The conditional factors indicate the length of time that a condition had existed before a suggestion was submitted.

Each criterion has been subdivided into intervals which in turn have been weighted or assigned a certain number of points (Section A in Table 4).

The savings table is prepared with monetary value for the savings achieved and the reward to be paid (section B in Table 4).

The method works as follows:

Section A

When a suggestion is evaluated, the points are allocated in accordance with the frequency of use and the length of time which the condition had existed. Points are allocated for A and then for B. The total of the combined points (i.e. A + B) are entered on the form.

Section B

Once the estimated annual savings have been calculated and located on the table, the total points (A + B) are located in the row under points awarded. Moving along the row of the saving we read down the appropriate column and find the reward amount. The following example illustrates the method:

A person earns a total number of four points if his suggestion is used more than 1000 times per year (2 points) and the problem had been in existence for more than two years (2 points) (Section A). If the annual savings are more than R10 000 we find this in the saving column (bottom line). The number of points (4 points, Section A) is found in column 4 of points awarded. Reading across from the savings column towards column 4 in points awarded we find R3 000 which is the reward amount.

The advantages of this type of suggestion reward are:

- It is summarised and user-friendly.
- It is simple and easily understood by the employees.

Table 4
AN EXAMPLE OF A VALUE TABLE FOR THE DETERMINATION OF COMPENSATION FOR CALCULATABLE SUGGESTIONS

SECTION A		
CRITERIA	POINTS	POINTS AWARDED
A. FREQUENCY OF USE (Number of times the suggestion is used per year)		
1. Less than 500 times.	0	
2. 500–999 times.	1	
3. 1 000 and more.	2	
B. CONDITION (The duration of the condition before the suggestion was submitted.)		
1. Less than one year.	0	
2. Between one and two years.	1	
3. More than two years.	2	
TOTAL POINTS (A + B)		
Note: Read off the award in the points awarded column below which corresponds with the total above.		

SECTION B					
SAVINGS	POINTS AWARDED				
	0	1	2	3	4
Up to 500	30	35	40	45	50
R501–R1 000	40	60	80	100	120
R1 001–R1 500	90	110	130	150	170
R1 501–R2 000	150	170	190	210	230
R2 001–R2 500	220	240	260	280	300
R2 501–R3 000	300	320	340	360	380
R3 001–R3 500	390	410	430	450	470
R3 501–R4 000	490	510	530	550	570
R4 001–R5 000	500	520	540	660	680
R5 001–R6 000	620	640	660	780	800
R6 001–R7 000	820	840	860	880	1 000
R7 001–R8 000	1 200	1 250	1 300	1 350	1 500
R8 001–R9 000	1 600	1 650	1 700	1 800	2 000
R9 001–R10 000	1 800	2 000	2 100	2 200	2 500
More than R10 000	2 000	2 200	2 400	2 600	3 000

- It is to a large degree objective.
- It specifies the maximum and minimum amounts which can be awarded.

16.2 Immeasurable suggestion rewards

Immeasurable suggestions have vested many problems for administrators and will probably continue doing so because of the subjectivity of the evaluation. Suggestors may become dissatisfied with the reward and this could demotivate them so much that they stop participating in the scheme.

Nevertheless, a number of methods are available which can be used with immeasurable suggestions. One method is to refrain from making a reward. The fact that the saving is immeasurable does not detract from its value to the organisation.

Another method is to treat each suggestion on its merits and to make ex gratia rewards based on the merits. Unfortunately, each person's sense of values is different, and this causes dissension.

Another approach is to determine the reward on the grounds of a number of criteria such as the degree of improvement, the level of ingenuity, initiative, creativity and the degree of relevance of the suggestion.

A reward form, together with the criteria, is then used to determine the applicable reward. Table 5 is an example of a tariff table. Although it is subjective in the sense that the criteria are interpreted by the evaluator, it is more acceptable than the other methods as it is founded on specific guidelines.

Another method is to categorise the immeasurable advantage in one of six categories which are each coupled to a specific rate. Table 6 illustrates this method.

A person who submitted a suggestion which is immeasurable but classified as very good, will thus receive R250 according to Table 6.

This method is also prone to the subjectivity of the responsible evaluator.

Table 5
TARIFF TABLE FOR IMMEASURABLE SUGGESTIONS

DATE: . . . . NAME AND NUMBER OF SUGGESTOR: . . . .

A LEVEL OF IMPROVEMENT

Minor	1, 2, 3, 4, 5
Reasonable	6, 7, 8, 9
Substantial	10, 11, 12, 13
Large	14, 15, 16, 17
Outstanding	18, 19, 20, 21, 22, 23, 24, 25, 26, 27, 28, 29, 30, 31, 32, 33, 34, 35

B LEVEL OF ORIGINALITY AND INNOVATION

Very little	1
Minor (use is made of an existing idea)	2
Reasonable (original idea but little innovation)	3
Considerable (new idea with a degree of innovation)	4
High (new idea with a lot of innovation)	5, 6, 7
Extremely ingenious (new concept with outstanding innovation)	8, 9, 10, 11, 12

C DEGREE OF RELEVANCE

Can be applied in only one department	1
Can be applied in all similar departments	2, 3
Can be applied throughout on a regional basis	4
Can be applied nationwide	5, 6, 7, 8, 9
Can be applied worldwide	10

TO CALCULATE THE VALUE OF THE REWARDS

Awarded for every point R . . . .

A × B × C × R = R . . . .

Maximum: 35 × 12 × 10 × R . . . . = R . . . .

Minimum: R . . . .

Table 6
AN EXAMPLE OF A CATEGORY TABLE FOR THE REWARD OF AN IMMEASURABLE SUGGESTION

CATEGORY TABLE

DATE: . . . .

EMPLOYEE'S NAME OR NUMBER. . . . .

CATEGORY	AMOUNT	ALLOCATION
Excellent	R300	
Very good	R250	
Good	R200	
Satisfactory	R150	
Reasonable	R100	
Adequate	R50	
Not applicable	0	

As is the case with measurable suggestions, a large number of variations can be used to arrive at an appropriate reward for an immeasurable suggestion. The selection of the method which will be used remains the responsibility of top management. According to the results of research, the points system is less acceptable to suggestors. The reason for this bias or prejudice was not identified.

16.3 Taxation on the compensation of suggestions

All financial rewards are subject to tax since it is regarded as part of the remuneration package. Taxation can be dealt with in two ways. *Firstly,* the employee has the tax deducted by the employer and paid to the Receiver of Revenue. The net result is that the reward is less than originally awarded because of the tax deduction. This has proved to be a negative factor and demotivational.

The *second* method is where the employer assumes the responsibility for the tax on the reward. Although the organisation appears to pay the tax, in actual fact the Receiver of Revenue pays a big portion of it. The reward paid is fully deductible since it is an expense incurred in the earning of income and is shown as an expense item. This effectively reduces the total taxable income by the reward plus tax. Once the reward is determined the tax due is calculated and added to the reward. The suggestor receives the total amount (reward plus tax) and the tax is then deducted and paid to the Receiver. The suggestor is left with a net amount which is equal to the full amount of the reward. The same system can also be used when supervisors share in the reward. This option has a motivational effect on the suggestor.

16.4 Speedy payment procedures

The evaluation process should be as short as possible in order to reduce the time between submission and reward. Although some delays are inevitable they can be reduced by using the following techniques:

- A pre-payment, based on, say, 50 % of the reward is paid within the first three months after the suggestion has been implemented. The remaining 50 % could be paid after one year. The first year's saving could be estimated during the evaluation of the suggestion. If the organisation's policy is to pay the suggestor 10 % of the net saving in the first year, then only 5 % will be paid out in the first three months and the remaining 5 % will be paid out after the suggestion has been on trial for a year and a more accurate net saving can be determined. There is thus an opportunity for the organisation to reconcile the estimated and actual net savings achieved. The spontaneity of management in making prepayment reflects its positive attitude toward the suggestion scheme.
- Authorisation to dispense rewards for minor suggestions is another method of reducing the delay. Where the amount of the reward is less than R50 (or any other ammount approved

by top management) it should not be necessary to verify the actual savings. The estimated saving is sufficient and can be used as a basis for the reward. Since a large number of suggestions fall into this category, the process can be shortened considerably.

- A third method aimed at shortening the period between submission and payment is to use a combination of the preceding methods. When it comes to minor suggestions, the estimated saving is sufficient ground for calculating the reward, whereas for larger amounts where 50 % of the total reward is paid within three months, the estimated net saving is used as a primary base and the actual saving achieved is used to determine the final amount at the end of the year.

Regardless of which method of reward calculation is used, all doubts must have been alleviated. The formulae or techniques should be communicated to the employees in order to generate understanding and trust in the system.

Whenever rewards are paid, as much publicity as possible should be given to the presentation. The result is two fold, in that the employee receives the recognition for his part but it also advertises and sells the suggestion system making participation more acceptable.

17. SUGGESTION SCHEME AND SMALL GROUP ACTIVITIES

A question which often arises is whether quality circles, or the so called small group activities can co-exist within an organisation. The answer to this question is unquestionably positive. Neither the small group/quality circle nor the suggestion system should fail because of the presence of the other. Both will maintain their own identities. It is also possible to channel many of the group ideas through the suggestion schemes.

In organisations which operate suggestion schemes without reward systems but instead offer other forms of recognition (for example a merit certificate or a trophy), it becomes relatively easy to accommodate both systems merely by operating the small group activities through the suggestion scheme.

However, the problem becomes more complex when the financial reward-type suggestion schemes are involved. The most obvious problems which need to be resolved are the idea theft and the distribution of the reward among the group.

Idea theft often occurs when a group member passes a group idea on to a non-member in return for a share in the reward which may be paid. A policy which restricts this type of practice can be introduced. The requirement is often that the group or individual record their suggestion prior to the commencement of the investigation in order to qualify for any reward.

Regarding the group as an individual overcomes the reward problem to a large degree. The reward is paid to the group as a whole and divided equally among the members, or devided as decided by the group members themselves.

Immeasurable saving suggestions complicates matters even further because the reward is not usually large. Dividing the amount among the group may result in a reward amount which is so small that all incentive to participate is dissipated. The problem becomes even more complicated when it comes to the division of the reward. If the group membership had remained constant throughout the period of the suggestion development the problem does not exist. However, when a member leaves the group in the investigative period or someone joins toward the end, the division problems are more complex.

One way of overcoming these problems is to establish a fund in which the reward is deposited for a certain length of time after which the funds are divided. Another alternative is to set a target amount and once the fund reaches that figure it is divided.

The following alternatives can be used:

- Accumulated funds can be used to sponsor events of the members.

- The accumulated funds can be donated to a selected welfare or charity organisation. Research has shown that this method finds favour with most groups.

The problem of dividing the rewards among group members can be averted if a predetermined policy has been laid down. The policy should stipulate, for example, that a member will be paid on a pro-rata basis according to the time spent on the project. If the policy is to pay out the funds after one year, the member who leaves after four months will receive one third of the reward at the end of the year. Similarly, the member who takes his place for the remaining eight months will receive two thirds of the reward.

In the short term, individuals will benefit more from the larger rewards than group members. However, because of the group's potential for submitting a larger volume of suggestions, the accumulated reward is likely to exceed that of the individual.

The focus of small group activities is to identify and solve problems through joint effort as opposed to the traditional suggestion scheme which focuses on the suggestion of the individual.

Groups need to meet on a regular basis to generate ideas, and this happens during normal working hours, whereas the individual develops his idea in his own time out of preference and for fear of idea theft.

The individual submits his suggestion with a solution to the scheme administrator while the group present their ideas personally or in writing to management. During the presentation the group make use of any means at their disposal, e.g., audiovisual aids, projectors and slides.

The drawback of small-group activities is that they are restricted to their immediate environment while the individual becomes a free agent and can submit ideas in any area he chooses as long as the end result benefits the organisation as a whole.

Suggestion schemes and small-group activities can live in harmony if certain ground rules are laid down.

Group suggestions should not be evaluated by the suggestion scheme personnel. The departmental manager should be the best person to evaluate the merits of the group's solution because of his involvement with the problem and the constant search for solutions.

Once the recommendations of the group have been accepted by management they can be transferred to the suggestion scheme for reward determination and payment.

If a suggestion scheme which offers financial rewards is in operation in an organisation, management should also consider including the group activity in the reward system. This will to a large extent reduce the threat of idea theft.

Included in the policy which deals with group activities should be a moratorium clause. It stipulates the period of time which a group is given to solve the problem. This clause gives them the sole right to solve the problem.

If, however, the group has actively concentrated on the problem but failed to solve it by the end of the moratorium, they should be given an extension of time provided the case has merit.

Possibly the single most important factor which may determine the success of both systems, separately or together, is the organisation's policy with regard to both systems. This policy should lay down clear guidelines which must serve as advice and guidance for all parties involved.

18. SUGGESTION SCHEME ASSOCIATIONS

18.1 The National Association of Suggestion Systems (NASS)

On July 27, 1942, a group of 35 interested suggestion administrators from different organisations met in Chicago to establish an association. Initially, the aim of the organisation was to establish a clearing house through which affiliated organisations could benefit from the experience gained by others in the field.

On 12 August 1942, with bylaws and the constitution completed, Ezra Taylor of the Pullman Company was elected the first president of NASS.

The first NASS conference was held in Chicago on 10 December 1942 and has been held annually since then. At the conferences special attention is paid to training. As the aims of the South African National Association of Suggestion Systems (SANASS) are similar to those of NASS, it will be discussed under the heading SANASS.

NASS headquarters are situated at:

230 North Michigan Avenue
Suite 1200
Chicago
ILLINOIS, USA, 60601
Telephone: (312) 372–1770.

Although most of the NASS members are from the United States of America, there are also international members in South Africa, England, Germany and Japan.

18.2 The South African National Association of Suggestion Systems (SANASS)

SANASS was established on May 15, 1990 to promote suggestion systems, which were almost non-existent in South Africa.

SANASS is a non-profit service organisation with the objective of promoting and improving suggestion systems and other worker-participation programmes.

The aims of the association are the following:

1. To collect and disseminate information, statistics, advice and materials about suggestion systems and similar concepts.
2. To enhance the quality of suggestion system administration by developing professional standards and programmes that will assist individuals to attain those standards and to certify those who maintain them.
3. To anticipate and identify world trends and patterns that could affect suggestion systems.

4. To keep abreast of research being done in the behavioral sciences and to translate this knowledge into useful information.
5. To develop and sponsor educational opportunities for the benefit of suggestion system administrators, top management and the public.
6. To inform commerce, industry, government and the public of the value and productive contributions of suggestion systems.
7. To provide opportunities for members and others to meet and exchange information, ideas and solutions to problems and to provide an authoritative counselling service to those interested.

In September 1990 SANASS affiliated with NASS which means that all NASS information is available to SANASS members. A list of addresses and telephone numbers of all NASS and SANASS members is available to members of the local association. This service makes overseas and local contacts possible.

SANASS presents an annual conference, mainly for training purposes and the exchange of knowledge and information. At the same time the annual general meeting takes place where new officials and a committee are elected.

Any inquiries can be addressed to:

SANASS
P.O. Box 1146
SILVERTON
0127

ANNEXURE 1

THE CONCEPTUAL POLICY DOCUMENT

1. THE NAME OF THE SCHEME

The organisation's suggestion scheme will be known as:

....

and will form part of the overall achievement improvement programme.

2. THE AIM OF THE SCHEME

The aim of the scheme is:

- ❑ To encourage employees to think creatively and constructively about their working environment;
- ❑ to draw employees' attention to cost savings and more efficient use of all resources;
- ❑ to develop a better relationship between the organisation and its personnel;
- ❑ to give employees the opportunity to participate in the improvement of the organisation as a whole;
- ❑ to foster a greater sense of loyalty amongst employees;
- ❑ to give employees the opportunity to supplement their incomes; and
- ❑ to improve the productivity and achievements of the organisation.

3. THE DEFINITION OF A SUGGESTION OR IDEA

A suggestion is an original, written proposal from an employee or a group of employees of an organisation, which aims to bring about an improvement in the methods, procedures, processes, use of equipment, quality of products and/or services, safety prevention measures, or a reduction in costs or the elimination of wastage, which will be to the advantage of the organisation..

4. TOPICS WHICH ARE NOT ELIGIBLE AS SUGGESTIONS

Suggestions concerning the following topics will not be considered:

- ❑ conditions of employment;
- ❑ salaries and fringe benefits;
- ❑ disciplinary and grievance procedures;
- ❑ matters which are the subject of current investigations.

5. THE SUGGESTION COMMITTEE

The suggestion committee will operate under the chairmanship of the . . . or his nominee, as well as co-opted members.

The permanent committee will comprise:

- ❑ The chairman: . . . .
- ❑ Secretary (Suggestion scheme co-ordinator): . . . .
- ❑ . . . .
- ❑ . . . .
- ❑ . . . .

The permanent committee has the right to co-opt the department head and supervisor of the suggestor or any other person who may be able to assist in the evaluation. The committee can also involve other experts for their opinions on the suggestion.

6. PARTICIPATION IN THE SCHEME

All employees of . . . .
are eligible to submit suggestions and will qualify for awards. Suggestions from non-employees will be accepted but will not qualify for awards.

7. SUGGESTION AWARDS

A suggestion will qualify for an award only if it results in an improvement in a current condition.

The basis of compensation is the following:

- ❑ Measurable or calculable suggestion:. . . . . . .% of the first year's net saving of which 50 % of the estimated net saving will be paid out after six months and the balance to be paid after 12 months or any stipulated period of time which will allow the suggestion to be comprehensively tested.
- ❑ The maximum reward for any *one* suggestion will not exceed the ammount of R . . . .
- ❑ Immeasurable suggestion: Minimum award will apply according to the tariff table (Annexure 1/1). The suggestion committee has the authority to grant a higher amount as an award if it is their opinion that the suggestion will contribute considerable towards productivity improvement.
- ❑ Supervisor award: The supervisor responsible for the suggestor concerned will receive . . . . % of the first year's net savings.

8. TAXATION ON THE SUGGESTION AWARDS

Taxation which is due on the award and should be paid by the recipient will be paid by the organisation. The full award plus tax will be paid to the suggestor who in turn will pay the taxable portion thereof to the Receiver of Revenue.

9. PROCEDURES RELATED TO THE SUBMISSION OF SUGGESTIONS

Suggestions must be submitted on the prescribed suggestion form (Annexure 1/2). The forms must be signed and correctly completed.

Suggestions may be forwarded through the mail or must be handed in personally to the suggestion office. The suggestion office will time and date stamp the form, and acknowledge receipt. A copy of the acknowledgement is sent to the suggestor.

Unsigned or incomplete suggestions will not be accepted. If it is necessary, the identity of the suggestor can be kept confidential except for the purposes of awards. Where necessary the committee may wish to interview the suggestor to clarify certain points.

The suggestion committee will meet monthly . . in order to evaluate suggestions. Based on information available, the suggestion committee may decide on the suggestions concerned, relating to:

- its feasibility for implementation;
- its rejection in which case a written notification will be sent to the suggestor, or
- further investigation and a subsequent evaluation in which case the suggestor will be informed.

10. THE RIGHT TO APPEAL

In the case where a suggestion has been turned down by the committee the suggestor has a right to appeal, provided that additional information or material which will support the appeal can be presented. The appeal must be lodged within a period of 12 months of date of rejection. No second appeals will be considered.

11. THE CESSION OF SUGGESTIONS

Suggestions which are accepted by the organisation become the sole property of the organisation. Ownership of the idea vests in the suggestor during the evaluation stage and an additional period of 12 months following the declining of the suggestion. If the suggestor wishes to prolong the period of ownership, he must complete the suggestion form and re-submit through the normal channels. This should be repeated for as long as the suggestor wishes to retain ownership. Any award stemming from the use of the idea must be given to the suggestor as long as he has retained ownership of the idea.

12. PATENTABLE SUGGESTIONS

Due to the cession of rights, the accepted suggestions become the sole property of the organisation and if the idea is patentable, the suggestor has no further claim on the organisation and any benefit resulting from the idea. Management can, as a gesture of goodwill, make and ex gratia award to the suggestor.

ANNEXURE 1/1
TARIFF TABLE FOR IMMEASURABLE SUGGESTIONS

DATE: . . . . NAME AND NUMBER OF SUGGESTOR: . . . .

A LEVEL OF IMPROVEMENT

Minor 1, 2, 3, 4, 5
Reasonable 6, 7, 8, 9
Substantial 10, 11, 12, 13
Large 14, 15, 16, 17
Outstanding 18, 19, 20, 21, 22, 23, 24, 25, 26, 27, 28, 29, 30, 31, 32, 33, 34, 35

B LEVEL OF ORIGINALITY AND INNOVATION

Very little 1
Minor (use is made of an existing idea) 2
Reasonable (original idea but little innovation) 3
Considerable (new idea with a degree of innovation) 4
High (new idea with a lot of innovation) 5, 6, 7
Extremely ingenious (new concept with outstanding innovation) 8, 9, 10, 11, 12

C DEGREE OF RELEVANCE

Can be applied in only one department 1
Can be applied in all similar departments 2, 3
Can be applied throughout on a regional basis 4
Can be applied nationwide 5, 6, 7, 8, 9
Can be applied worldwide 10

TO CALCULATE THE VALUE OF THE REWARDS

Awarded for every point R . . . .

A × B × C × R = R . . . .
Maximum: 35 × 12 × 10 × R . . . . = R . . . .
Minimum: R . . . .

The following pages (87, 89, 91, 93) show and example of a suggestion form to be completed in quadruplicate. On the reverse sides of the form are the evaluation form (page 90) and the most important rules of the system (pages 88, 92 and 94).

ANNEXURE 1/2
SUGGESTION FORM (Part I)
(The suggestion office — file alphabetically)

Complete in quadruplicate.

	FOR OFFICE USE ONLY
Name:	Suggestion No.: . . . .
Department:	Original suggestion: . . . . . .
Division/section:	Appeal: . . . .
Supervisor:	Individual suggestion: . . . . .
Tel. No.:	Group suggestion: . . . .
Personnel No.	Subject of suggestion: . . . . .

Note:
I/we accept the provisions set out in the suggestion scheme policy.

Signature: . . . .

THE PROBLEM:
(Describe the present problem, method process or procedure)

. . . .

A PROPOSED SUGGESTION
(Describe in detail. Include additional pages if the space provided is insufficient.)

. . . .

. . . .

NATURE OF IMPROVEMENT: (Tick what is applicable.)

Time saving: . . . . ☐ . . . . hours
Financial saving: . . ☐ . . . . rands
Generated income: ☐ . . . . rands
Immeasurable: ☐

Departments/divisions that will be affected by the suggestion:

. . . .

. . . .

FOR OFFICE USE ONLY:
Date received: . . . .
Time received: . . . .

PROCEDURES RELATED TO THE SUBMISSION OF SUGGESTIONS

Suggestions must be submitted on the prescribed suggestion form. The forms must be signed and correctly completed.

Suggestions may be forwarded through the mail or must be handed in personally to the suggestion office. The suggestion office will time and date stamp the form, and acknowledge receipt. A copy of the acknowledgement is sent to the suggestor.

Unsigned or incomplete suggestions will not be accepted. If it is necessary, the identity of the suggestor can be kept confidential except for the purposes of awards. Where necessary the committee may wish to interview the suggestor to clarify certain points.

The suggestion committee will meet monthly . . in order to evaluate suggestions. Based on information available, the suggestion committee may decide on the suggestions concerned, relating to:

- its feasibility for implementation;
- its rejection in which case a written notification will be sent to the suggestor, or
- further investigation and a subsequent evaluation in which case the suggestor will be informed.

THE RIGHT TO APPEAL

In the case where a suggestion has been turned down by the committee the suggestor has a right to appeal, provided that additional information or material which will support the appeal can be presented. The appeal must be lodged within a period of 12 months of date of rejection. No second appeals will be considered.

SUGGESTION FORM (Part II)
(The office — for evaluation)

Complete in quadruplicate.

FOR OFFICE USE ONLY
Suggestion No.: . . . .
Original suggestion: . . . . . .
Appeal: . . . .
Individual suggestion: . . . . .
Group suggestion: . . . .
Subject of suggestion: . . . . .

Note:
I/we accept the provisions set out in the suggestion scheme policy.

Signature:

THE PROBLEM:
(Describe the present problem, method process or procedure)

. . . .

A PROPOSED SUGGESTION
(Describe in detail. Include additional pages if the space provided is insufficient.)

. . . .
. . . .

NATURE OF IMPROVEMENT: (Tick what is applicable.)
Time saving: . . . . ☐ . . . . hours
Financial saving: . . ☐ . . . . rands
Generated income: ☐ . . . . rands
Immeasurable: ☐

Departments/divisions that will be affected by the suggestion:

. . . .
. . . .

FOR OFFICE USE ONLY:
Date received: . . . .
Time received: . . . .

EVALUATION FORM
(Please return to suggestions office)

Date of evaluation: . . . .

Application area of the suggestion:

- Only own department/section: ☐
- Applicable to entire department ☐
- Also applicable to other departmer ☐

Was the problem/bottleneck previousiy noted? Yes ☐ No ☐

If so, when, and what were the results?

. . . .

. . . .

. . . .

. . . .

Must the suggestions be implemented? Yes ☐ No ☐

If so, when can they be implemented? . . . .

Are further tests, research or other actions necessary? Yes ☐ No ☐

If so, when can a decision be expected? . . . .

Briefly state that reasons for acceptance, rejection or postponement.

. . . .

. . . .

. . . .

. . . .

. . . .

SUGGESTION FORM (Part III)
(The suggestion office — file according to subject)

Complete in quadruplicate.

Name: . . . .
Department: . . . .
Division/section: . . . .
Supervisor: . . . .
Tel. No.: . . . .
Personnel No. . . . .

FOR OFFICE USE ONLY
Suggestion No.: . . . .
Original suggestion: . . . . . .
Appeal: . . . .
Individual suggestion: . . . . .
Group suggestion: . . . .
Subject of suggestion: . . . . .

Note:
I/we accept the provisions set out in the suggestion scheme policy.

Signature: . . . .

THE PROBLEM:
(Describe the present problem, method process or procedure)
. . . .

A PROPOSED SUGGESTION
(Describe in detail. Include additional pages if the space provided is insufficient.)
. . . .
. . . .

NATURE OF IMPROVEMENT: (Tick what is applicable.)
Time saving: . . . . ☐ . . . . hours
Financial saving: . . ☐ . . . . rands
Generated income: ☐ . . . . rands
Immeasurable: ☐

Departments/divisions that will be affected by the suggestion:
. . . .
. . . .

FOR OFFICE USE ONLY:
Date received: . . . .
Time received: . . . .

SUGGESTION AWARDS

A suggestion will qualify for an award only if it results in an improvement in a current condition.

The basis of compensation is the following:

- ❑ Measurable or calculable suggestion:. . . . . . .% of the first year's net saving of which 50 % of the estimated net saving will be paid out after six months and the balance to be paid after 12 months or any stipulated period of time which will allow the suggestion to be comprehensively tested.
- ❑ The maximum reward for any *one* suggestion will not exceed the amount of R . . . .
- ❑ Immeasurable suggestion: Minimum award will apply according to the applicable tariff table. The suggestion committee has the authority to grant a higher amount as an award if it is their opinion that the suggestion will contribute considerable towards productivity improvement.
- ❑ Supervisor award: The supervisor responsible for the suggestor concerned will receive . . . . % of the first year's net savings.

PATENTABLE SUGGESTIONS

Due to the cession of rights, the accepted suggestions become the sole property of the organisation and if the idea is patentable, the suggestor has no further claim on the organisation and any benefit resulting from the idea. Management can, as a gesture of goodwill, make and ex gratia award to the suggestor.

SUGGESTION FORM (Part IV)
(The suggestor — notice of acceptance)

Complete in quadruplicate.

Name:	*FOR OFFICE USE ONLY*
Department:	Suggestion No.: . . . .
Division/section:	Original suggestion: . . . . . .
Supervisor:	Appeal: . . . .
Tel. No.:	Individual suggestion: . . . . .
Personnel No.	Group suggestion: . . . .
	Subject of suggestion: . . . . .

Note:
I/we accept the provisions set out in the suggestion scheme policy.

Signature: . . . .

THE PROBLEM:
(Describe the present problem, method process or procedure)

. . . .

A PROPOSED SUGGESTION
(Describe in detail. Include additional pages if the space provided is insufficient.)

. . . .

. . . .

NATURE OF IMPROVEMENT: (Tick what is applicable.)
Time saving: . . . . ☐ . . . . hours
Financial saving: . . ☐ . . . . rands
Generated income: ☐ . . . . rands
Immeasurable: ☐

Departments/divisions that will be affected by the suggestion:

. . . .

. . . .

FOR OFFICE USE ONLY:
Date received: . . . .
Time received: . . . .

THE DEFINITION OF A SUGGESTION OR IDEA

A suggestion is an original, written proposal from an employee or a group of employees of an organisation, which aims to bring about an improvement in the methods, procedures, processes, use of equipment, quality of products and/or services, safety prevention measures, or a reduction in costs or the elimination of wastage, which will be to the advantage of the organisation..

TOPICS WHICH ARE NOT ELIGIBLE AS SUGGESTIONS

Suggestions concerning the following topics will not be considered:

- conditions of employment;
- salaries and fringe benefits;
- disciplinary and grievance procedures;
- matters which are the subject of current investigations.

THE CESSION OF SUGGESTIONS

Suggestions which are accepted by the organisation become the sole property of the organisation. Ownership of the idea vests in the suggestor during the evaluation stage and an additional period of 12 months following the declining of the suggestion. If the suggestor wishes to prolong the period of ownership, he must complete the suggestion form and re-submit through the normal channels. This should be repeated for as long as the suggestor wishes to retain ownership. Any award stemming from the use of the idea must be given to the suggestor as long as he has retained ownership of the idea.

ANNEXURE 2

INTRODUCTION AND CONTINUAL AWARENESS PROGRAMMES

Regardless of how well employees accept and participate in a suggestion system, awareness and reinforcement are most important factors for success. It becomes a continual marketing exercise where the target is the employee and the product is the suggestion scheme and as in any marketing drive, innovations are required to keep employees informed and involved.

The three main objectives of an awareness programme are:

- To inform employees of the objectives, procedures, policy and advantages of the scheme. This is especially important during the introduction of the new scheme;
- to gain the confidence and the co-operation of the employees; and
- to encourage and stimulate employees to become creative thinkers constantly aware of the need for improvement.

An awareness programme has a number of options and techniques which can be used to great effect. The most popular methods are discussed below, but it is important to note that they can be used individually or in conjunction with other techniques. The emphasis must be on the communication of the message with maximum retention.

1. BROCHURES

A brochure is very useful in explaining the suggestion scheme, especially to new personnel. During the induction and orientation programme, new staff members are normally overloaded with new information. Because of the volume of information, a large percentage of it is lost. A brochure is thus helpful in furnishing or confirming information and it can always be referred to at a later date.

A colourful, well illustrated brochure containing sketches, diagrams and cartoons all designed to convey information is generally very affective. Without being too lengthy, the brochure should contain at least the following information:

- The name of the scheme;
- definition of the suggestion scheme;
- definition of the suggestion;
- procedures to follow when submitting a suggestion; and
- how an award is determined.

2. POSTERS

Posters must be used with caution. In practice, posters lose their effectiveness because they are placed in strategic positions and forgotten. The employees become used to these posters and tend to ignore them totally. Posters should be changed around often in order to keep employees guessing as to what is coming next. Another danger is that posters are overloaded with information and the impact is lost. A poster should comprise a minimum amount of text and a maximum visual impact. Because the impact of posters is relatively cheap to accomplish, they are an ideal medium when a specific reaction is required. For example, if senior management wishes to invite suggestions related to safety, then posters can be used effectively to achieve this end.

Posters can achieve much more than a thousand words, provided they are used correctly. Posters are basically used to influence the attitudes and behaviour of employees and to refresh their memories.

In order to be more effective, posters should form an integral part of a specific programme. The poster programme also requires constant attention and planning. The following guidelines should aid in the effectiveness of a poster programme.

The positioning of posters

- As far as is possible, posters should be placed at EYE LEVEL.

- Place posters in strategic positions where people walk past or gather, for instance the cafeteria or tea room.
- Posters should not be placed between other notices or advertisements.
- The lighting should be good since it takes a person approximately three seconds to walk past a poster.
- Avoid placing posters together; rather spread them out.
- A poster which is framed will attract more attention than an unframed poster. (Suggestion: Whenever frames are used, use a type where the contents are easily replaced).
- Posters which are exposed to weather conditions should be fully protected.
- If a glass covering is used, it must be non-reflective or the glass should be tilted forward to minimise reflection.

Replacement of posters

To ensure that posters do not become part of the background or 'wallpaper', it is suggested that posters be changed around every 14 days and, where possible positioned elsewhere.

3. CIRCULARS

Circulars are a relatively cheap but effective medium for creating awareness. The best results are normally achieved where the circular is sent by the chief executive officer. These letters are especially useful when attempts are being made to elicit suggestions on a specific topic, e.g. safety awareness.

Compilers of circulars are cautioned not to use examples to illustrate ideas. Suggestors will use these examples as basis for their own ideas and not give their creativity free reign.

4. THE IN-HOUSE NEWSPAPER

Using the in-house newspaper can have a greater impact than a circular because employees prefer reading the newspaper to circulars. The suggestion articles usually evoke a lot of interest and are widely discussed among the employees.

The newspaper is an ideal medium for stimulating and developing the confidence of the employees. Photographs of award ceremonies serve to illustrative the value which management places on the programme. Publicity given to the awards and tokens has a more stimulation effect than other means. It is a cheap method of spreading news and obtaining publicity.

5. NOTICES

Notices which appear on NOTICE BOARDS are cheap and have a reasonable impact, but they do have their shortcomings. A single notice often 'disappears' among the other notices on the same board and reduces its impact value. The chances are very remote that a specific notice on an overly full board will be seen. This applies to posters as well. Replacement notices should be planned as an ongoing exercise and the replacement should vary from the previous one.

Notices can also be distributed in the form of HANDBILLS which is a more expensive medium with less impact because employees do not read them. It is often regarded as just another advertisement or junk mail.

Many organisations have the facility available for a message to appear on the SALARY SLIP. This is also relatively cheap and has a great impact because workers will often regard and accept it as a personal message. Reminders can also take the form of 'BUMPER STICKERS' and be distributed to the employees. It is a relatively expensive medium but in general it will have a better impact than hand-bills for example, because its life-span is longer. There is a tendency to overlook stickers over a period of time.

6. EXHIBITIONS

Exhibitions of accepted suggestions require a great deal of work and normally have a low success rate when aiming to encourage employees to submit suggestions. The reason for this is due to the fact that most personnel are aware of the successful suggestions.

Where exhibitions relate to areas beyond the working environment and attract the broader public, they have a higher prestige value which can motivate employees to participate in the suggestion scheme.

Exhibitions should be understandable and stimulating in order to generate interest. The setting up of exhibitions should be left to the experts to achieve the maximum result.

In most cases, the more successful exhibition are one-off in nature and the time spent on them is relatively short. Permanent exhibitions tend to lose their impact because people become used to them. A static exhibition has less impact than one which is in constant motion.

7. COMPETITIONS

Competitions are widely used to stimulate interest. The following competitions or variations are commonly used:

- The highest number of accepted suggestions per person, department or section during a given time period. A trophy and/or a prestigious financial award normally motivates submission of suggestions.
- President's award/senior management award for the suggestion which contributed the most benefit to the organisation during a given period of time, be it financial savings or safety of some nature. An ex gratia financial award and/or a prestigious trophy should be offered as a prize.
- Theme competitions can be run over a period of time, say six months, with a specific prize on offer. In order to be considered for the prize, the suggestions must be submitted within the period and must be about the theme or topic. The

competition is run over and above the normal suggestion scheme. The competition can be used to focus on problems or problem areas in the hope that a solution will emerge.

- Inter-departmental competitions can be held using the following criteria:
  - The number of suggestions submitted per 10 or 100 workers;
  - the percentage of accepted suggestions;
  - the average financial value per suggestion;
  - the average saving for the accepted suggestion.

  The department or section which wins will receive an additional financial award which can be shared amongst the personnel or a floating trophy which can be displayed.

The supervisor or manager plays a key role in the success of the competition by providing direction, encouragement, advice and where necessary help with the refinement of suggestions.

Competitions should enjoy maximum publicity and exposure in the in-house news paper, regional press and regional radio services such as regional news and journal programmes.

8. AUDIOVISUAL AIDS

Audiovisual aids such as closed circuit television, slide programmes with sound tapes, film programmes and film flashes also have an impact. It must be remembered that audiovisual aids are an expensive medium to use for communication. However, audiovisual aids are very successful when used in conjunction with static displays.

9. HONOUR ROLL

A Roll of Honour placed in a conspicuous place, such as a conference room, committee room or cafeteria will also draw the attention of employees to the suggestion scheme. Employees whose names appear on the roll of honour must have made a major contribution or achievement, for example, a suggestion wich resulted in a net saving of more than R1 million during the first year after implementation. The roll has a twofold purpose, recognising the contributions and motivating the employee corps as a whole. However, the roll of honour should be maintained regularly.

10. ACHIEVEMENT BOARDS

Achievement boards in the form of graphs, for example, that display the achievement for a specific division, department or production unit will also attract attention. The information displayed on these boards must be current and reflect the latest data. Competition between departments, divisions or business units will be stimulated by these boards. If the information is stale or the boards are hidden, the impact is lost.

11. CLOSING REMARKS

A suggestion scheme can be dynamic and exciting, with a vitality of its own which can be achieved by using intensive publicity programmes.

An awareness programme at the commencement of a new scheme is essential. Potential suggestors, i.e. the entire work force, must be informed as to what the programme entails, what it holds in store for the employee and what is in it for the organisation right from the outset of the programme.

A publicity programme is just as important for an old established suggestion scheme as it is for a new one. Employees need to be reminded to use the suggestion scheme. Repeated demands should be made on the thoughts and idea powers of the employees.

The publicity programme must emphasise the awards and prize-winning ceremonies. Employees must see that something is happening. If the scheme appears to ignore suggestions or appears to be dormant the employees will lose interest. A good publicity programme is absolutely necessary to ensure success.

ANNEXURE 3

THE SUBMISSION OF SUGGESTIONS

In order to facilitate and expedite the evaluation process, suggestions should be submitted according to the procedure below.

1. THE SUGGESTION FORM

Suggestions will be considered for evaluation only if they are submitted on the prescribed suggestion form (refer to annexure 1/2). The suggestion form is available from the secretary of the suggestion committee or the scheme's co-ordinator.

Employees may submit as many suggestions simultaneously as they like, provided that each suggestion is recorded on a separate suggestion form.

All suggestion forms must be signed. Anonymous suggestions will not be accepted for evaluation. Even where a group submits a suggestion, all its members' names must appear in Part I of the form and it must be signed by every member.

The suggestion form must be completed in quadruplicate and all four copies (Part I–IV) must be submitted to the secretary of the suggestion committee. Part I, which contains personal details, is used by the suggestions office for registration purposes and is filed alphabetically according to the suggestor's name. The first copy (Part II) on which the personal details are not legible on the front and reverse sides, is sent to the suggestions committee for evaluation. The results of the evaluation are shown on the reverse side. Part III, the second copy, is filed in the suggestions office according to its subject, while the final copy (Part IV) serves as acknowledgement of receipt and is returned to the submitter.

The suggestion form must be completed fully, except where *'office use'* is indicated. Where diagrams and sketches form part of the suggestion, they should be attached to the suggestion form.

2. CONFIDENTIALITY

The identity of suggestors will be regarded as strictly confidential in order to protect suggestors and suggestions. The suggestors may personally decide whether or not to discuss the suggestion with his supervisor before he submits it. If the suggestor decides to discuss the suggestion with his supervisor, the supervisor must assist instead of opposing the suggestion.

Even if the suggestor decides to bypass the supervisor, the latter may still become involved with the evaluation of the suggestion, in which case the supervisor will not know the identity of the suggestor.

The suggestor's identity will also remain unknown to the evaluation committee before or during evaluation. Only the suggestions office will, for administrative purposes, be aware of the suggestor's identity.

3. THE PLACE OF SUBMISSION

All suggestions must be sent to the secretary of the suggestion committee. They can be handed in personally or they may be submitted through the internal post.

4. ACKNOWLEDGEMENT OF RECEIPT

Acknowledgement of receipt will be sent within five working days of receipt of the suggestion. A short letter, signed by the chief executive or his appointee, in which the suggestor is thanked for his effort and is encouraged to submit further suggestions, should be attached to part IV of the suggestion form.

5. SUGGESTION ADMINISTRATION

The areas designated for *'office use'* must be completed by the scheme office. A suggestion number will be allocated and the form is dated and time-stamped and the receipt is recorded.

Figures 1, 2 and 3 indicate the registers that must be completed.

Figure 1
THE NUMBER REGISTER (IN A CHRONOLOGICAL ORDER)

Suggestion Number	SUGGESTOR			Receipt		
	Name	Position	Department	Date	Time	Subject

Figure 2
THE NAME REGISTER (ALPHABETICAL)

Suggestor	Suggestion Number	Subject	Suggestion		Date Handled	First Year's Estimated Savings	Amount of Award
			Accepted	Rejected			

Figure 3
THE SUBJECT REGISTER (ALPHABETICAL ACCORDING TO SUBJECT)

Subject	Suggestion Number	Suggestor	Date submitted	Date concluded

The registers can be manually operated or computerised. It is important to note that the registers should be kept up to date at all times. It also serves as the main source of information for the monthly report.

ANNEXURE 4

THE EVALUATION AND AWARDING OF SUGGESTIONS

1. THE SUGGESTION COMMITTEE

All suggestions will be evaluated by the suggestion committee. This committee will consist of a permanent committee and a number of co-opted members. The permanent committee usually comprises four members. It is essential that a member of top management is chairman of the permanent committee. This indicates the commitment of senior management to the suggestion scheme. The suggestion scheme manager/co-ordinator assumes the role of secretary of the permanent committee. As a rule, the other two permanent members are any of the following: a representative of the financial department, the production manager and an industrial engineer.

The permanent committee can co-opt the suggestor's departmental head and his immediate supervisor. The committee may also co-opt other personnel who have knowledge of the suggestion subject-matter.

The evaluation of a suggestion should be completed within THREE months and the suggestor must be informed of the outcome within the same period. If the suggestion is not evaluated within the stipulated time, monthly progress reports should be issued to the suggestor on a continuous basis.

2. EVALUATION STAGES

The various stages in the evaluation process are diagrammatically illustrated in figure 2 on page 59 above.

3. GUIDELINES FOR EVALUATION

The following guidelines should be borne in mind by the evaluation committee:

- ❑ Always be receptive, objective and fair. Do not be susceptible to the negative influence of others.

- Regard all suggestions received as feasible until proven otherwise.
- A correlation exists between the number of submitted suggestions and the delay in providing feedback to the suggestor. The longer the time taken to provide feedback, the smaller the number of submitted suggestions. Feedback time must be reduced to the shortest time.
- Record the dates on which different information is received. This maintains order and logic throughout the evaluation.
- Although it is not the responsibility of the evaluators, effort should be made to ensure that idea theft does not occur. The submitted suggestion should be as a result of the suggestor's own initiative.
- The evaluator's task is to collect information, to obtain results and to test the idea in practice in order to determine if the results are correct. The evaluator should not, under any circumstances, be influenced by his own opinions.
- The evaluators should not allow themselves to be influenced by the negative attitude of any person before the investigation has been completed. Once the evaluation has been completed all aspects, whether positive or negative, will be evaluated.

Once all the information has been collected and analysed by the evaluators, the evaluation committee must decide whether or not the suggestion is acceptable. All these details are recorded on the reverse side of Part II of the evaluation form. The secretary will deal with the matter further (submissions to top management, process the suggestion and perform all the necessary administrative procedures).

4. THE REWARDING OF SUGGESTIONS

Management should not be under the misapprehension that suggestors are trying to win competitions. On the contrary, the suggestor has provided extra inputs with which he hopes to increase his income or gain recognition in some way. The suggestors earn the extra compensation or recognition. Once the suggestion has been accepted, the award or recognition should be paid/given with the minimum of delay.

The award for tangible suggestions is . . . per cent of the first year's net savings. Fifty per cent of the estimated net savings must be paid six months after the suggestion has been implemented. The adjusted balance must be paid 12 months after implementation. An adjusted balance means half of the estimated net saving less all further costs and expenses that were not taken into account in the actual calculation. The maximum reward for any ONE suggestion will not exceed the amount of R . . . .

In the case of immeasurable suggestions, the compensation will be determined from a rate table. The minimum amount paid for an immeasurable suggestion will be R . . .. Because no savings can be calculated, the compensation awarded to the suggestor must be paid within one month of the implementation of the suggestion.

The suggestor's immediate supervisor will be entitled to supervisor's compensation which is . . . per cent of the first year's tangible saving. In the case of non-calculable suggestions, the supervisor will receive the equivalent of 40 % of the amount compensated to the suggestor. The payment of supervisor's commission occurs in the same manner or time period as that of the suggestor.

The organisation will assume responsibility for the tax payments due on the award. After the compensation is determined, the taxation is calculated and added to the award. The suggestor thus receives the award as well as the taxation thereon. When the actual payment is made, only the award portion is paid out while the tax is paid to the Receiver of Revenue in the form of PAYE. This procedure also applies to the reward paid to the supervisor.

5. GROUP SUGGESTIONS

In spite of the fact that a suggestion was submitted by a group of employees who had all signed the suggestion form, the group will be regarded as an individual and treated accordingly. Only one award cheque will be issued. Unless otherwise decided by the members participating, the first person named in the suggestion will be considered for taxation purposes.

The manner of sharing the award amongst the group members is a mutual decision and management accepts no responsibility for this.

6. DECLINED SUGGESTIONS

Management should take cognizance of the fact that approximately 75 % of all suggestions received will be declined. It is extremely important that declined suggestions are treated with care. Rejections which are mishandled could discourage further submissions.

Within seven days of the suggestion being turned down, the scheme manager should:

- ❑ Advise the suggestor of the results giving the full reason why it was not accepted and thanking him for his efforts; and
- ❑ personally hand the letter to the suggestor at the same time discussing the suggestion to emphasise the interest which management has in the scheme. The suggestor should be encouraged to submit further suggestions.

7. THE RIGHT TO APPEAL

The suggestor is only entitled to appeal once and the appeal must be submitted in writing within twelve months of the suggestion being rejected.

The suggestor will be advised when to appear personally before the suggestion committee to support the suggestion and to supply additional information and/or material. This additional information and/or material will be added on the existing suggestion form for re-evaluation.

The suggestion committee meeting at which the suggestor should appear should take place within one month after receiving the written appeal at the suggestion office.

8. PATENTABLE SUGGESTIONS

Accepted suggestions become the property of the organisation. The suggestor has no further right to the benefits which may arise from the suggestion.

Suggestions which, in the opinion of the suggestion committee, have patentable possibilities, may be referred to the relevant authorities for patent rights and evaluation without the consent of the suggestor, who will not be liable in any way for any costs. It will be registered in the name of the organisation and will remain the property of the organisation.

Management has agreed to offer, as an incentive for patentable ideas, to pay the suggestor, over and above the normal award, an amount equivalent to the royalties received during the first 12 months, provided the suggestor is still in the employ of the organisation.

9. EVALUATION OF THE SUGGESTION SCHEME PROGRAMME

Top management should, after a reasonable lapse in time, evaluate the system to determine whether the scheme has been successful and whether it came up to expectations.

For this purpose, the suggestion scheme evaluation questionnaire (Annexure 4/1) is completed periodically, at least once per year, by the employees. All employees will be asked to complete it — or it can be done on a random selection basis.

The questionnaire can also be used for another purpose. If it appears that a specific department is not participating, the questionnaire may be used to determine whether the supervisor is

ANNEXURE 4/1

Strictly Confidential

SUGGESTION SCHEME EVALUATION QUESTIONNAIRE

Name: . . . . Personnel Number: . . . . . .

Department: . . . .

Division/Section: . . . . Telephone Number: . . . . . .

Supervisor: . . . .

Notes:

1. The success of the suggestion scheme programmes depends on the employees. Therefore, your sincere personal comments are very important.
2. All information supplied by you will be treated as confidential and will be handled only by the suggestion scheme office. Identification is necessary should we require additional information.

1.	How long have you been employed by this organisation?	☐ Years ☐ Months
2.	Are you aware of the existence of the suggestion scheme?	Yes ☐ No ☐
3.1	Have you submitted any official suggestion since you began working at the organisation?	Yes ☐ No ☐
3.2	If so, how many?	☐
4.1	Have you submitted any official suggestions during the past 12 months?	Yes ☐ No ☐
4.2	If so, how many?	☐
4.3	How many of these suggestions were adopted and have received recognition?	☐
5.1	Have you attended any suggestion award ceremony since you began working at this organisation?	Yes ☐ No ☐
5.2	If so, how many?	☐
5.3	Have you attended any suggestion award ceremonies during the past 12 months?	Yes ☐ No ☐
5.4	If so, how many?	☐
6.1	Do you consider the suggestion scheme programme a success?	Yes ☐ No ☐

6.2 If not, where would you say the problem lies? . . . .
. . . .

6.3 In your opinion, how can the suggestion scheme programme be improved? . . . .
. . . .
. . . .

providing all the necessary information and assistance regarding the scheme.

The departmental heads, as well as senior management, should receive a report back at least once a month regarding the administration of the suggestion scheme. The suggestion scheme report form (Annexure 4/2) is used for reporting purposes. The existence of the report should be made known. At both meetings, some or other action should be taken as a result of the report, for example:

> 'Send congratulations to the department that submitted the most suggestions, or decide that in the following months, special attention will be given to safety suggestions, or that a special competition is being run, etc.'

Senior management as well as departmental heads should feel constantly committed to and show interest in the programme. This remains the cornerstone of the success of the suggestion scheme programme.

ANNEXURE 4/2
REPORT FOR THE MONTH/YEAR . . . . 19 . . .

REPORT ITEMS	CURRENT MONTH/YEAR		CORRESPONDING PERIOD FOR PREVIOUS YEAR	
1. The number of suggestions received				
2. The number of suggestors who participated in the scheme				
3. The number of suggestions evaluated				
4. The average time to process a suggestion				
5. The number of accepted suggestions				
6. The number of rejected suggestions				
7. The total amount of paid awards				
8. The average award per suggestion				
9. The total cost of keeping the programme running				
10. The total estimated first year's savings for adopted suggestions				
11. The average savings per adopted suggestion				
12. The least single award payment				
13. The highest award payment				
14. The total amount paid for tangible suggestions				
15. The total amount paid for intangible suggestions.				

Select Bibliography

Alexander, W. 1982. *Suggestions are alive and well at U.S. Steel.* Annual Industrial Engineering Conference proceedings. pp 377–383.

Anthony, W.P. 1978. *Participative Management.* Reading, Massachusetts: Addison-Wesley Publishing Company. p 214.

American Productivity Center. 1980 Suggestion Program integrates support / recognition, produces high returns. *Case Study 13, Honeywell, Incorporated.* Houston: American Productivity Center. 3 p.

American Productivity Center. 1981. Suggestion Plan decentralization yields greater involvement. *Case Study 16, Phillips Petroleum Company.* Houston: American Productivity Center. 4 p.

American Productivity Center. 1982. Techniques to spruce up the suggestion box. *The Productivity Letter,* Vol 1 no 6, pp 1–3.

Beach, D.S. 1980. *PERSONNEL — The management of People at Work.* Fourht Edition. New York — Macmillan Publishing Co., Inc. 714 p.

Bergerson, A.W. 1977. Employee suggestion plan still going strong at Kodak. *Supervisory Management,* vol 22, May 1977, pp 32–36.

Blekkink, G.J. 1981. *Mensen en ideen.* Second Revised Edition. Netherlands: Ideeëncentrum. 112 p.

Clark, J. 1977. Want to start your own program? Here are a few suggestions. *Iron Age,* 6 June 1977, p 55.

Clutterbuck, D. 1978. Soviet Union taps shop-floor talents. *International Management,* vol 33, May 1978 pp 53–54.

Dewar, D.L. 1979. *Quality Circles.* Red Bluff: Quality Ciicles Institute. 48 p.

Dewar, D.L. 1980a. *The Quality Circle Guide to Participation Management.* New York: Prentice-Hall 414 p.

Dewar, D.L. 1980b. *The Quality Circle Handbook.* Red Bluff: Quality Circle Institute. p F1.1–F 23. 12.

Flippo, E.B. 1980. *Personnel Management.* Fifth Edition Tokyo: McGraw-Hill Kogakusha, Ltd. 511 p.

Goodman, P.S. 1982. Why Productivity Programs Fail: Reasons and Solutions. *National Productivity Review,* vol 1, no 4 pp 369–380.

Goodwin, J.S. 1983. Productivity improvement: Where do you start? *Production Management,* vol 5, no 2, pp 35 -41.

Greenlaw, P.S. 1980. Suggestion systems: an old approach to a new problem. *The Personnel Administrator,* January 1980, pp 49–54.

Kawasaki steel Corporation. 1980. *The TG Activities Manual.* Tokyo: Technical Control Department, Kawasaki Steel Corp. 54 p.

Marx A.E. 1986. *Wenkeskemas se bydrae tot produktiwiteitsverhog-ing: 'n Teoreties-empiriese studie, 1984.* (Unpublished DCom-dissertation, University of Pretoria) 450 p.

Moore, B.E. and Ross, T.L. 1978. *the Scanlon Way to Improve Productivity: A Practical Guide.* New York: John Wiley & Sons. 228 p.

Myers, D.W. & Archer, E.R. 1978. When the Suggestion Box Fails. *Personnel,* vol 55.September / October 1978, pp 37–42.

National Association of Suggestion Systems. (NASS). 1980. Suggestion Systems, An Answer to Perennial Problems. Reprint from *Personnel Journal.* Costa Mesa, California: A.C. Croft, Inc. 6 p.

National Association of Suggestion Systems (NASS), 1983. Management: Participation . . . Support . . . Involvement. *NASS-PAK,* Second Quarter, 1–6.

Ollsen, K. 1976. Suggestion Schemes Seventies Style. *Personnel Management,* vol 8, no 1, pp 36–39.

Reuter, V.G. 1976(a). Suggestion Systems and the Small Firm. *American Journal of Small Business*, vol 1, no 2, pp 37–46.

Reuter, V.G. 1976. A New Look at Suggestion Systems. *Journal of Systems Management*, vol 27, pp 6–15.

Reuter, V.G. 1977. Suggestion Systems — Utilization, Evaluation, and Implementation. *California Management Review*. vol 19, no 3, pp 78–89.

Sandell, R.M. 1979. Promoting employee suggestions. *Supervision*, vol 41, July 1979, pp 11–13.

Sayles, L.R. & Strauss, G. 1981. *Managing Human Resources*. Second Edition. Englewood Cliffs: Prentice-Hall, Inc. 510 p.

Scheer, W.E. 1979. *Personnel Administration Handbook*. Second Edition. Chicago: Dartnell Press, 1088 p.

Seinwerth, H.W. 1948. *Getting Results from suggestion plans*. First Edition. New York: McGraw-Hill Book Company, Inc. 223 p.

USA 1981. Profitable Turnaround of a Limping Suggestion Program. *National Productivity Report*, vol 10, no 9 May 15, pp 1–2.

Waring, A.B. 1959. *People and Productivity, A Practical Guide for Administrators*. London: British Productivity Council. 95 p.

Weimer, G.A. 1977. Hang up this profit center: A Suggestion Box. *Iron Age*, 6 June 1977, pp 49–55.